OVER A RED-HOT STOVE

Frontispiece. 1806 advertisement for Henry Marriott's patent jack. This mechanism is set up here to run two horizontal spits and three dangle-spits. Despite its name, no patent exists for Marriott's jack. Sarah Sophia Banks Collection, BM 85.95. Photograph courtesy of the British Museum. See pp. 99–124 below.

OVER A RED-HOT STOVE

ESSAYS IN EARLY COOKING TECHNOLOGY

LEEDS SYMPOSIUM ON FOOD HISTORY
'FOOD AND SOCIETY' SERIES

edited by
IVAN DAY

PROSPECT BOOKS
2009

First published in 2009 by Prospect Books, Allaleigh House, Blackawton, Totnes, Devon TQ9 7DL.

Based on papers from the nineteenth and twentieth Leeds Symposia on Food History, April 2004 and April 2005, 'Open Hearth Cookery' and 'Baking: from Cereal Crops to Oven-baked Goods', with two additional chapters. This is the fourteenth volume in the series 'Food and Society'.

© 2009 as a collection, Prospect Books (but © 2009 in individual articles rests with the individual authors).

The authors assert their right to be identified as the authors of their several pieces in accordance with the Copyright, Designs & Patents Act 1988.

No part of this publication may be reproduced, stored in a retrieval system, or transmitted in any form or by any means, electronic, mechanical, photocopying, or otherwise, without the prior permission of the copyright holder.

BRITISH LIBRARY CATALOGUING IN PUBLICATION DATA:
A catalogue entry for this book is available from the British Library.

ISBN 978-1-903018-67-5

Typeset by Tom Jaine.

Printed and bound by the Cromwell Press Group, Trowbridge, Wiltshire.

CONTENTS

Illustrations and Acknowledgements	6
Notes on Contributors	12
Foreword *C. Anne Wilson*	13
Introduction *Ivan Day*	15
Chapter 1 Cast Iron Progress – The Development of the Kitchen Range *David J. Eveleigh*	19
Chapter 2 Ox Roasts – From Frost Fairs to Mops *Ivan Day*	55
Chapter 3 The Roast Beef of Windsor Castle *Peter Brears*	83
Chapter 4 The Clockwork Cook – A Brief History of the English Spring-jack *Ivan Day*	99
Chapter 5 Barms and Leavens – Medieval to Modern *Laura Mason*	125
Chapter 6 Baking in a Beehive Oven *Susan McLellan Plaisted*	149
Bibliography	157
Index	161

ILLUSTRATIONS

Frontispiece.
    1806 advertisment for Henry Marriott's patent jack (British Museum)

1. A typical eighteenth-century roasting range from Powell's *Complete Book of Cookery*, c.1770 — 18
2. Kitchen grate with cast-iron uprights and adjustable cheeks from Heathfield Hall, Handsworth, Birmingham — 21
3. A close-up view of the large roasting range dating from 1809 at Bucklebury Manor, Berkshire — 21
4. In the kitchen at Betchworth House, Surrey — 22
5. Cast-iron oven made by the Benthall Foundry, Coalbrookdale, Shropshire — 22
6. Trade card of Underwood & Co., furnishing ironmongers in Bristol from c.1812–1828 — 25
7. The stewing stove from Sir John Vanbrugh's 'Designs for Kings Weston', Gloucestershire, 1717 (reproduction is courtesy of Bristol Record Office) — 25
8. Thomas Robinson's patent range and oven, 1780 — 26
9. An open range from an undated catalogue probably dating to the 1840s of the Coalbrookdale Company, Shropshire (photograph by courtesy of the Ironbridge Gorge Museum Trust Library) — 26
10. William Nicholson's 'Newark Cottage Range' of 1848 — 29
11. The original range in the kitchen of Sir John Soane's house, Lincoln's Inn Fields, London (photograph by courtesy of Sir John Soane's Museum) — 29
12. An open range in a cottage near Congresbury, North Somerset supplied by Harris & Kingdom, Bristol ironmongers from 1885 to 1944 — 30
13. Plan and elevation of the brick stove designed by Count Rumford and fitted in the kitchen of the Baron de Lerchenfeld, Munich in about 1794 — 30
14. A typical closed range with a single oven and boiler from a Coalbrookdale catalogue of 1875 (The Ironbridge Gorge Museum Trust Library) — 33

15.	A closed range with oven, boiler and hot closet from J.H. Walsh's *Manual of Domestic Economy*, 1857	33
16.	A convertible range from the Coalbrookdale catalogue for 1875 (The Ironbridge Gorge Museum Trust Library)	34
17.	A very typical large range of the 1890s – the 'Swinton' – a convertible range patented by Hattersley in 1890	37
18.	The 'KB' range by Coalbrookdale, 1911 (The Ironbridge Gorge Museum Trust Library)	38
19.	The 'Cosmopolitan Cooking Range'	38
20.	The 'Yorkshire Gas Kitchener', a combination range for coal and gas, manufactured by Beverley and Wylde of the Leeds Gas Stove Works, 1882	39
21.	An 'Eagle Range' with its unmistakable strap work ornament and eagle trade mark	39
22.	The 'Gem' portable range manufactured by Brown and Green 1882	40
23.	A closed range of 1892 made by J.D. Young & Son	40
24.	An open range from the undated Coalbrookdale catalogue of *c.*1840–50 (The Ironbridge Gorge Museum Trust Library)	43
25.	A typical north-country range at an unknown location in Cumbria, photographed *c.*1900 (Museum of English Rural Life)	43
26.	A 'Yorkshire' open range from the Coalbrookdale catalogue of 1875 (The Ironbridge Gorge Museum Trust Library)	44
27.	Kitchen at Rookhope, Stanhope, Durham, late nineteenth century (Beamish, The North of England Open Air Museum)	44
28.	Land army girls sitting by a Cornish range in 1918 (Royal Cornwall Museum, Truro)	48
29.	A tin bath and bucket in front of an open range at Brierley Cottages, Sutton in Ashfield, Nottinghamshire (courtesy of Nottinghamshire Local Studies and www.picturethepast.org.uk)	48
30.	Detail from a contemporary broadside illustration of the 1714/15 London frost fair	54

31.	Detail from a broadside illustration of the 1683/84 London frost fair (British Museum)	54
32.	Detail from a broadside of the 1683/84 London frost fair (British Museum)	57
33.	Jan Griffier the Elder, *The London Frost Fair* of 1683/84 (whereabouts unknown)	57
34.	George Cruickshank, *London Frost Fair*, etching, 1838 (British Museum)	58
35.	Nikolaus Hogenberg, *Ox being roasted in the streets of Bologna during the coronation procession of Charles V*, etching, 1530 (British Museum)	58
36.	Detail from printed broadside, 1814 (British Museum)	61
37.	Ox roast at Batley Carr, Yorkshire, celebrating the diamond jubilee of Queen Victoria in 1897	61
38.	Plate used at Batley Carr ox roast, 26 June 1897	62
39.	Plate used at an 1885 ox roast to celebrate the royal assent for the Manchester Ship Canal Bill	62
40.	Ox paraded on a cart on its way to being roasted in the town of Patricroft in 1885 (courtesy of Salford Library)	66
41.	The Oldham miners' strike medallion of 1858 (photograph courtesy of Mark Smith)	67
42.	Ox roast in Tamworth at a town pageant in 1913	70
43.	Oxen roasting at a hospital thanksgiving day at Windsor in 1872	70
44.	Postcard of a bullock being roasted at a mop fair in Stratford-upon-Avon	73
45.	Postcard of an early twentieth-century mop fair ox roast in Stratford-upon-Avon	73
46.	A postcard illustration of an early twentieth-century mop fair pig roast in Stratford-upon-Avon	74
47.	Detail of a postcard illustration of two butchers carving a roast ox at an early twentieth-century Stratford-upon-Avon mop fair	74
48.	A three-hundredweight baron of beef and sixty fowls roasting in the London Guildhall kitchen for Lord Mayor's Day, steel engraving from *The Illustrated London News*, 13 Nov. 1887	76

49.	The bringing-in of the baron, steel engraving from *The Illustrated London News*, 13 Nov. 1887	76
50.	The Lord Mayor's baron is carved in ritual fashion, steel engraving from *The Illustrated London News*, 13 Nov. 1887	79
51.	A full baron of beef being roasted with a mechanical dangle-spit for the 1903 Christmas dinner at the Constitutional Club in London, *Illustration*, Paris, 26 December 1903	79
52.	Roast goose day (29th September) at the Old Men's Hospital in Norwich, steel engraving from *The Illustrated London News*, 8 Oct. 1859	80
53.	The roasting ranges at Hampton Court, *c.*1530, and Kew Palace, *c.*1735? (drawings by Peter Brears)	85
54.	The great kitchen, Windsor Castle, from a watercolour by J. Stephanoff, *c.*1820 (drawing by Peter Brears)	86
55.	The kitchen of Windsor Castle in 1856, from the west	86
56.	The kitchen in 1857, from the west, with the roasting hearth on the east wall (drawing by Peter Brears)	89
57.	A baron of beef in the western roasting hearth of Windsor Castle kitchen, after a painting by Frank Watkins, 1870s (drawing by Peter Brears)	90
58.	Illustration of roasting range in Windsor Castle kitchen from the *Pictorial World*, 2 January 1875	93
59.	The Windsor Castle kitchens in 1894, from the east	93
60.	The western roasting range with Christmas roasts, 1894	94
61.	The western roasting range, with its smoke hood and roasting screen, after a photograph of 1898 (drawing by Peter Brears)	94
62.	Anatomy of a common weight-jack: (a) woodcut illustration from Joseph Moxon, *Mechanick Exercises or the Doctrine of Handy-Works* (London, 1678); (b) a two-spindle English iron weight-jack dating from the late eighteenth century (photograph courtesy of David Hansord)	98
63.	Detail of an advertisement for John Joseph Merlin's *Rotisseur Royal* of 1773 (Courtesy of Science Museum)	101

64. An early illustration of a weight-jack from John Wilkins, *Mathematical Magic* (London, 1648)   102
65. (a) An English weight-jack with a brass fore-side engraved 'THO:/WILLS/ST AUSTLE' (drawing by Peter Brears); (b) illustration of a French weight-jack, Antoine Gogué, *Les Secrets de la cuisine Française* (Paris, 1856); (c) pulley system for a common weight-jack, Thomas Webster, *An Encyclopaedia of Domestic Economy,* New Edition (London, 1847); (d) a detail from the trade card of T. Ward, Ironmonger of 25 Newgate St., London, *c.*1782 (British Museum)   103
66. Roasting range formerly in the kitchen of Chatsworth House (© Devonshire Collection, Chatsworth. Reproduced by permission of Chatsworth Settlement Trustees)   105
67. Steam roasting-jack 1806 (photograph courtesy Intellectual Property Office)   106
68. (a) Advertisment of Edmund Lloyd, ironmonger, 1801 (British Museum); (b) smoke-jack formerly in the kitchen of Lowther Castle (photograph Private Collection)   109
69. Handbill advertising Joseph Merlin's inventions 1781–3 (photograph courtesy of Science Museum)   110
70. Advertisement for Joseph Merlin's *Rotisseurs Royal c.*1773 (British Museum)   113
71. (a) Joseph Merlin's 'ventilator movement'; (b) Joseph Merlin's flywheel with meat hooks; (c) a design for a smoke-jack by Joseph Braithwaite (1795) (Intellectual Property Office)   113
72. Joseph Merlin's *Rotisseur* movement (Intellectual Property Office)   114
73. (a) *Molinello con tre spedi,* from Bartolomeo Scappi, *Opera* (Venezia, 1570); (b) a Dutch spring-jack; (c) a *molinello* in use in a Renaissance kitchen, from Bartolomeo Scappi, *Opera* (Venezia, 1621)   114
74. Anatomy of a Renaissance spring-jack: (a) *Machina*

	da voltar, from Pietro Zonca, *Novo teatro di machine ed edificii* (Padova, 1607); (b) a late seventeenth-century Italian *voltaspiédo* with a mainspring/fusee movement	117
75.	William Lane's design for the movement for his improved spring-jack of 1821 (Intellectual Property Office)	117
76.	John Pearse's improved spring-jack of 1822: (a) Pearse's original design (Intellectual Property Office); (b) in later versions of his jack, Pearse's spit took this form (drawing by Peter Brears); (c) a version of Pearse's jack with two spits, Elizabeth Hammond, *Modern Domestic Cookery*, sixth edition (London, 1824)	118
77.	A horizontal spring-jack and screen, Eliza Acton, *Modern Cookery* (London, 1845)	121

NOTES ON CONTRIBUTORS

PETER BREARS was formerly Director of Leeds City Museums. He is one of Britain's leading social historians of food and as consultant to the National Trust and other bodies has supervised the restoration of many of Britain's most important period kitchens, including those of Petworth and Belvoir Castle. His publications include *Great Food in Yorkshire 1650–1750*, *The Old Devonshire Farmhouse* and *Cooking and Dining in Medieval England*.

IVAN DAY is a food historian with a special interest in re-creating the food of the past in period settings. His work has been exhibited at the Museum of London, the Getty Museum, the Bard Graduate Center, Waddesdon Manor and Hillwood Museum, Washington DC. He is the author of *Cooking in Europe 1650–1850*. He lives and runs practical courses on period cookery in the English Lake District.

DAVID J. EVELEIGH is the Curator of the Black Country Living Museum. He was formerly Curator of Social History at Blaise Castle House Museum, Bristol and is the author of several books, including *Firegrates and Kitchen Ranges*, *Old Cooking Utensils* and *A History of the Kitchen*.

LAURA MASON is a food historian and regular contributor to the Leeds Food Symposium. Her publications include *Traditional Foods of Britain* (with Catherine Brown), *Sugar Plums and Sherbet* and *Farmhouse Cookery*.

SUSAN McLELLAN PLAISTED is the proprietress of Heart to Hearth Cookery, a food history business in Bucks County, Pennsylvania. She is the coordinator of the foodways programme at Pennsbury Manor, the re-created home of William Penn. Through her business she offers courses in hearth cooking and baking, and provides lectures, demonstrations and programme sat many historic sites in the USA. She was a contributor to the *Oxford Encyclopedia of Food and Drink in America*.

FOREWORD

C. Anne Wilson

This book was inspired by two one-day symposia of the Leeds Symposium on Food History held in York in 2004 and 2005 and titled 'Open Hearth Cookery' and 'Baking: from Cereal Crops to Oven-baked Goods' respectively. Four of the chapters are based directly upon talks given at those two meetings. Of the remaining two, one has been contributed by Peter Brears and the other, on the subject of outdoor ox-roasts, has been added by Ivan Day himself.

At our Symposium on 24 April 2004 we also heard Sally Grainger speak on Roman cookery carried out over hot ashes, and in the afternoon she gave us a practical demonstration in the courtyard of nearby Fairfax House. In an adjacent area John Hudson showed us how to recreate some historic English recipes cooked over a chafing dish; while at our indoor venue Ivan offered us hands-on inspection of original spits and other hearth furnishings from earlier centuries.

At our Symposium on 16 April 2005 the first speaker was John Letts who told us about the wheat varieties of late medieval England, some of which are still grown in remote parts of Spain and Turkey. He had sourced seedcorn from there, and now cultivates the same cereals in southern England and tests the resultant flour in baking. Later, Malcolm Thick spoke about the types of bread in regular use in eighteenth-century England; and we also heard the talks by Laura Mason and Susan McLellan Plaisted, on which their chapters in this book are based, and another one by Ivan Day entitled 'Pies, pasties and pastry.'

Previous volumes in this series 'Food and Society' have been issued as follows:

1. *'Banquetting Stuffe': the Fare and Social Background of the Tudor and Stuart Banquet*, ed. C.A. Wilson (1986 Symposium), 1991.
2. *The Appetite and the Eye: Visual Aspects of Food and its Presentation within their Historic Context*, ed. C.A. Wilson (1987 Symposium), 1991.
3. *Traditional Food East and West of the Pennines*, ed. C.A. Wilson (1988 Symposium), 1991.
4. *Waste Not, Want Not: Food Preservation in Britain from Early Times to the Present Day*, ed. C.A. Wilson (1989 Symposium), 1991.
5. *Liquid Nourishment: Potable Foods and Stimulating Drinks*, ed. C.A. Wilson (1990 Symposium), 1993.
6. *Food for the Community: Special Diets for Special Groups*, ed. C.A. Wilson (1991 Symposium), 1993.
7. *Luncheon, Nuncheon and Other Meals*, ed. C.A. Wilson (1992 Symposium), 1994. Now republished in paperback as *Eating with the Victorians* (Sutton, 2004).
8. *The Country House Kitchen, 1650–1900: Skills and Equipment for Food Provisioning*, ed. P.A. Sambrook and P. Brears (double volume for 1993 and 1994 Symposia), 1996.
9. *The Country House Kitchen Garden, 1600–1950: How Produce was Grown and How it was Used*, ed. C.A. Wilson (1995 Symposium), 1998.
10. *Feeding a City: York*, ed. E. White (double volume for 1997 and 1998 Symposia), 2000.
11. *Food and the Rites of Passage*, ed. L. Mason (1999 Symposium), 2002.
12. *The English Cookery Book*, ed. E. White (2001 Symposium), 2004.
13. *The English Kitchen*, ed. E. White (2003 Symposium), 2007.

The first six volumes were published by Edinburgh University Press and are now out of print; the following three by Sutton Publishing (two of them in association with The National Trust); the volumes from no. 10 have been published by Prospect Books.

INTRODUCTION

Ivan Day

This book is based on papers presented at the seventeenth Leeds Symposium on Food History, but also contains two supplementary essays. In addition to the lectures, the day's activities included a handling session of period cookery equipment kindly made possible by the staff of the York Castle Museum. A number of original period spitjacks, spits and other objects relating to hearth cookery were examined at close quarters.

Before the television set usurped its role during the mid-twentieth century, the kitchen hearth was the main focus of family life. It was not only the place where food was cooked, but also the main gathering point where tales were told, clothes dried and cold hands warmed. It is too easily forgotten that the Latin word focus means 'hearth' or 'fireplace'. Human beings have been drawn to the 'focus' since the very earliest times as a centre for the exchange of ideas. Without it, our development as a social species would not have been the same.

In terms of food preparation the hearth was a converging point for countless activities. Not only were meat and fish broiled over the embers and roasted in its radiant heat, but dough was proved in its warmth and bread toasted in front of its flames. Generations of nameless cooks have toiled in the heat of the fireplace and it is from their almost infinite pool of experience that the art and technology of cookery emerged.

In the papers given here, David Eveleigh sets the scene by considering the development of the kitchen range. From the early modern period to the rise of gas and electricity he shows how the range allowed the key cooking activities of roasting, boiling and baking to be carried out in a single place. He demonstrates how the evolution of the range reflected that of the wider industrial revolution. Early ranges were designed and made by artisan blacksmiths, but as the Enlightenment unfolded, important inventors, master iron founders and cooks turned their attention to improving this essential domestic appliance. His paper is illustrated with numerous photographs and images, many of them published here for the first time.

Perhaps the most archetypal 'focus' of all is that of the outdoor bonfire. Food cooked by the heat of an open air blaze is an elemental form of cookery enjoyed by all. Camp-fire cookery still retains its powerful appeal as a kind of culinary ancestor worship in the guise of the modern barbecue. One heroic type of outdoor cookery formerly used to celebrate key local and national events was the roasting of entire oxen. Ivan Day examines this ancient tradition and traces its roots to charitable events and fairs where very large numbers of people required feeding. He considers its social history and shows how a material culture emerged as the practice was used in the nineteenth century, not just for celebrating occasions like royal jubilees, but also for canal openings and even miners' strikes. His essay is illustrated with many rare broadside woodcuts, early photographs and objects that have never been published before.

Peter Brears moves our attention from the ox roast in the street to the culture surrounding the royal baron of beef in the palace kitchen. He focuses on the kitchens of Windsor Castle and illustrates the development of the royal roasting ranges from the time of Edward II to the Great War. By the middle of the eighteenth century the 'royal baron of beef' had become a sacred symbol of national unity, and the English roasting cook treated this gargantuan cut of meat with the reverence it deserved. Cookery on such a vast scale required a specialist technology and a highly organised kitchen staff. The smoke-jacks at Windsor and the skilled cooks who used them were second to none.

Proceeding from this, Ivan Day turns his attention to the clockwork devices once commonly employed in this country for open fire roasting. These 'culinary robots' were among the first labour-saving devices to appear in the early modern period kitchen and transformed the working lives of many kitchen servants. He offers a basic taxonomy of the various kinds, but examines in detail the evolution of one type in particular, the wind-up spring-jack. Like the development of the kitchen range, the story of this device demonstrates the increasing ingenuity of inventors, clockmakers and entrepreneurs as the early Industrial Revolution unfolded. Once an expensive item found only in the kitchens of the wealthy, cheap spring-driven jacks eventually made roasting technology possible even in the humble cottage kitchen.

If the Roast Beef of Old England was the chief celebration dish of a nation of cattle farmers, wheaten bread was its principal staple. To make good bread, the baker needed yeast, which we now know to be a living organism, but which our ancestors saw as a mysterious substance with almost supernatural powers, thus one of its early names, 'Godes good'. Laura Mason addresses the history of barms and leavens and illuminates how these essential ingredients were strongly linked to that other important British domestic activity, the brewing of malt liquors. She traces the history of leavening agents, from the Anglo-Saxon *beorma* skimmed from the surface of fermenting ale, to nineteenth-century chemical substitutes, such as pearl ash and hartshorn.

Once the dough had been been proved, preferably in a warm place near the hearth, there would be no bread without an oven. In the final chapter, Susan McLellan Plaisted discusses some of her own practical experience of baking in historic wood-fired ovens in the United States. One of the first ovens to be used in America was a clay oven brought from England by the early Jacobean settlers of Jamestown. She goes on to show how other equipment, techniques and baking recipes from the Old World influenced the baking practices of early colonists .

Time and space did not allow an examination of many other facets of hearth cookery and this publication cannot pretend to be a complete guide to what is an enormous subject.

Figure 1. A typical eighteenth-century roasting range from Powell's Complete Book of Cookery, *c.1770.*

CHAPTER ONE

CAST-IRON PROGRESS –
THE DEVELOPMENT OF THE KITCHEN RANGE

David J. Eveleigh

The cast-iron, coal burning cooking range was the essential Victorian kitchen fitting but it was always more than just a cooker. The range was a vital part of the home: a source of warmth and comfort and a favourite place to sit by. It was usually the only source of hot water and the obvious location in many households for the weekly bath. Laundry irons were heated on the range, and in the countryside, in harsh weather at lambing time, near-dead lambs could be revived by its warmth. The range is often fondly remembered for the warm cosy atmosphere it created in the kitchen and the cheerfulness of its fire. But not all memories are so favourable. There was the unavoidable dirt involved in lighting the fire and of even more when it was routinely cleaned. Clearing the soot from the flues, which might be a weekly task, and the chore of polishing the range with black lead is recalled by some as 'a nightmare'. Then there was the frustration of oven flues that would not draw – of smoky chimneys – and the discomfort of encountering a range in use on a hot summer's day.

Whilst the kitchen range might be associated in the popular mind with Victorian Britain, its origins stretch back to the sixteenth and seventeenth centuries. Its development was shaped by two materials which underpinned eighteenth- and nineteenth-century technology, coal and cast-iron. In 1861, Isabella Beeton (1836–65) stated, 'without fuel a kitchen may be pronounced to be of little use'.[1] Fuel was critical. Virtually everyone cooked by a fire and it was the choice of fuel that determined the type of fireplace. Wood or turf could be burned directly on the open hearth but coal required an iron container – a grate – if it was to burn effectively. By the early 1600s, some kitchen grates were already termed 'ranges'. These were simple structures of wrought iron, but all later ranges – from the late eighteenth century onwards – were made largely of cast-iron. Much of the subsequent development of the range was shaped not by those who had to cook by them but the men who made them, the iron founders.

The relationship between coal and the grate is confirmed in several different types of records. The most compelling evidence survives in the thousands of surviving probate inventories which indicate that where coal was cheap and easily available, grates soon replaced the open hearth. As early as 1568, the Yorkshire inventory of the goods and chattels of Thomas, Lord Wharton of Healaugh records that he had '20 lode' of coal in his 'wodyerd' and '2 iron chymneys' in the house – one in the hall and the other in the kitchen. In 1637, Robert West of Knaresborough had coals in his coal house and 'one iron rainge' in the hall.[2]

Across the country, in south Gloucestershire, coal was mined locally and, again, inventories suggest this led to the widespread adoption of grates. In the published inventories for Frampton Cotterell and district covering the period 1539–1804, the earliest record of a grate occurs in the 1618 inventory of Thomas Gyles, a husbandman of Winterbourne. The series reveals that by the end of the century grates were common in the area.[3] The published inventories for several Shropshire parishes around modern-day Telford show the same close relationship between the availability of locally mined coal and the use of grates.[4] In towns the shortage of wood – and, therefore, its expense – encouraged the use of coal. By the seventeenth century, seaborne coal from Newcastle was widely used in London. Coal smoke was a feature of life in London by the time of the Restoration, when we find Samuel Pepys (1633–1703) recording improvements to his range in 1661:

> And so home – where I find all clean and the harth and range, as it is now enlarged, set up; which pleases me very much.[5]

Where wood or turf remained the usual fuels, then the open hearth remained general. This is borne out by the series of inventories for Writtle in mid-Essex where grates are only recorded five times in the period 1635–1747. The dependence on wood fuel in mid-eighteenth century Essex is corroborated by Pehr Kalm, a Swedish botanist who visited England in 1748. Heading towards Essex, he noted that although coal was the common fuel in London, it gave way to wood no more than fourteen miles outside the city.[6] Forty years later in August 1788, another keen observer of ordinary things – this time an English aristocrat – the Honourable John

CAST-IRON PROGRESS

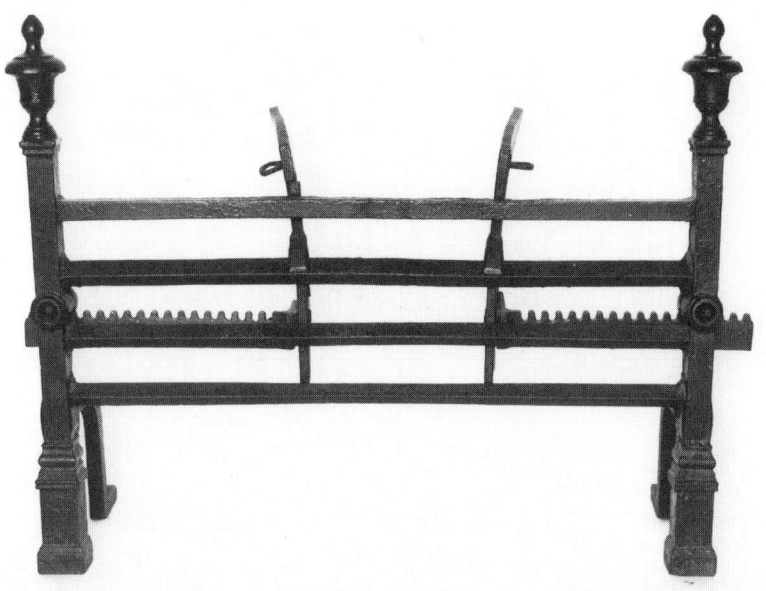

Figure 2. Kitchen grate with cast-iron uprights and adjustable cheeks from Heathfield Hall, Handsworth, Birmingham, built by James Watt in 1790. It is just over 40 inches wide.

Figure 3. A close-up view of the large roasting range dating from 1809 at Bucklebury Manor, Berkshire.

Figure 4. In the kitchen at Betchworth House, Surrey, an eighteenth-century 'perpetual' oven made by the Carron Company shares the fireplace opening with a range of much later date. The oven is complete with firebox, flues and soot doors. Although the oven door appears at first glance to be octagonal it is actually a hexagon opening outwards from its bottom edge. It is decorated with classical figures in fine quality cast relief, typical of the company's late eighteenth-century ovens and grates.

Figure 5. Cast-iron oven made by the Benthall Foundry, Coalbrookdale, Shropshire and supplied by Underwood & Co. of Clare Street, Bristol, to 5 Harley Place in nearby Clifton about 1815; their oval brass plate is fixed to the oven door above the bust of Admiral Howe. The three brass handles around the edge operate a soot scraper fixed to the oven roof.

Byng (1743–1813) wrote this whilst staying in the Red Lion in Bodiam,

> At our last inn [the Queen's Head, Hawkshust], and in this part of the county, they used a wood fire, as most of the kingdom did when wood was plenty; a common cook here would not know how to manage a coal fire.[7]

Occasionally diaries record the actual moment when the age-old wood burning open hearth was replaced by a coal burning grate. For example, Thomas Turner (1729–93) a shopkeeper in East Hoathly Sussex records in his diary for Thursday, 22 April 1756 that he borrowed a bushel and a half of 'sea coal'. The next day he wrote, 'This day I had a fire-grate set up'.[8]

However, some parts of the south of England were to retain the open hearth until the coming of the railways in the mid-nineteenth century and even later. Writing on the rural economy of Devon in 1808, Charles Vancouver bemoaned the, 'unnecessary consumption of wood' in the open fireplaces of farmhouses. He pointed out that the waste might be 'diminished by the introduction of Count Rumford's cottage ovens or some other equally and perhaps more appropriate contrivance.' Vancouver might have been disappointed if he could have known that open hearth cooking was to survive in some isolated farmhouses and cottages in Devon until as late as c.1950. There were scattered instances of the open hearth surviving into the twentieth century in other southern counties such as Hampshire and Berkshire.

From the 1840s, the opening of railways in rural districts widened the availability of coal. In the mid-nineteenth century, the Dorset dialect poet William Barnes (1801–86) mourned the passing of the old open hearth in his poem, *The Settle an' the Girt Wood Vire*,

> But they've a-wall'd up now wi' bricks
> The vier pleäce vor dogs an' sticks
> An only left a little hole
> To teäke a little greäte o' coal,
> So small that only twos or drees
> Can jist push in an' warm their knees.[9]

In the far south-west, the diary of one small Cornish farmer, James Stevens (1847–1918) who farmed at Zennor, west of St Ives, records the transition from the open hearth to a coal-burning range at the end of the nineteenth century. His diary records with almost monotonous regularity the perpetuation of a very ancient part of the farming calendar across much of upland western Britain: the cutting of thousands of turfs and hundreds of faggots of furze every spring and summer which were then stored in ricks. The task consumed much of Stevens' time in between the sowing of oats – his main crop – in April and the harvest in August. A typical diary entry, for 23 May 1892, reads, 'Cut 20 faggots of furze in great croft'. Then in 1897 Stevens moved to a farm a few miles further west at Sancreed, south of Penzance. The cutting of turf and furze disappears from his diary and on 16 October that year his diary contains the following brief entry. 'At Penzance on horseback for knobs for slab. 'Slab' was the Cornish name for a range. His diary begins to record frequent purchases of coal and in December he records, one suspects somewhat ruefully, 'At Penzance for 6 cwt coal, this makes 16 cwt we have had in Sancreed [i.e. since the move to Sancreed on 30 September 1897].' By 30 March 1898, he had purchased two tons of coal at a cost of 11d per cwt.[10]

As Mrs Beeton had observed, fuel was the vital factor in the kitchen and the relationship with coal was fundamental and critical to the development of the kitchen range. The ironworkers – smiths, founders and ironmongers – who shaped the development of the range over two hundred years were chiefly concerned with improving fuel efficiency and later on with reducing smoke emission. The range, therefore, was always a chimney fireplace first, a cooker second. It was to take an American, Benjamin Thompson, Count Rumford (1753–1814) to expose the absurdity of this.

Early grates were made chiefly of wrought-iron and not cast-iron. It is often suggested that the very first were made by joining two large firedogs – or andirons – as typically used on the open hearth with horizontal fire-bars. This is quite feasible but a note of caution should be introduced here: some of the free-standing 'basket grates' surviving today probably date to no earlier than the early twentieth century when fireplaces in some period properties were restored to their presumed original state. However, seventeenth-century inventories indicate that grates were commonly used with firedogs. Thus the 1698 inventory of Margaret Smyth, a widow of Westerleigh in south Gloucestershire, records, 'a pittgrate, the Cast back. Two Basting ladles and an old firegrate and a paire of Dogges'.[11] The basting ladles confirm that this was a cooking fireplace and regularly used for roasting. The spit was probably supported by hooks on the firedogs which would have stood either side of a free-standing grate. There was also an

CAST-IRON PROGRESS

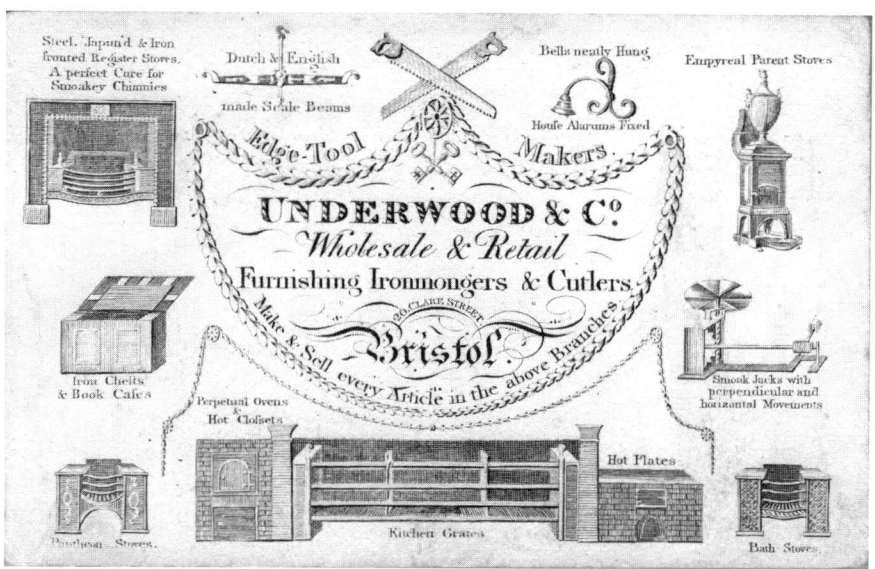

Figure 6. Trade card of Underwood & Co., furnishing ironmongers in Bristol from c.1812-1828. Their premises were in Clare Street, then containing some of Bristol's finest shops. The kitchen grate depicted on the card is flanked on the right by a hot-plate set in brickwork and on the left by a perpetual oven although hot-closets were also available.

Figure 7. The stewing stove from Sir John Vanbrugh's 'Designs for Kings Weston', Gloucestershire, 1717. (Bristol Record Office)

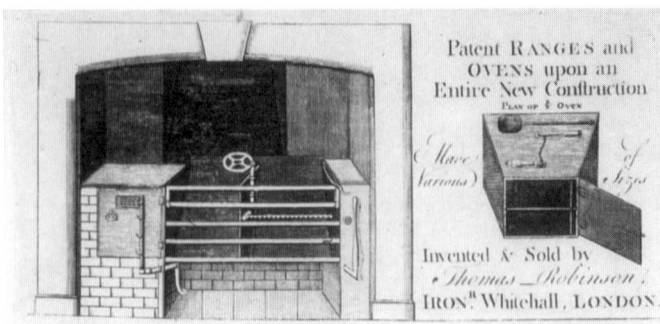

Figure 8. Thomas Robinson's patent range and oven, 1780. The grate is fitted with one adjustable cheek which winds in from the right so that the fire is always in contact with the oven on the left. This is the earliest known depiction of a kitchen range made with an oven.

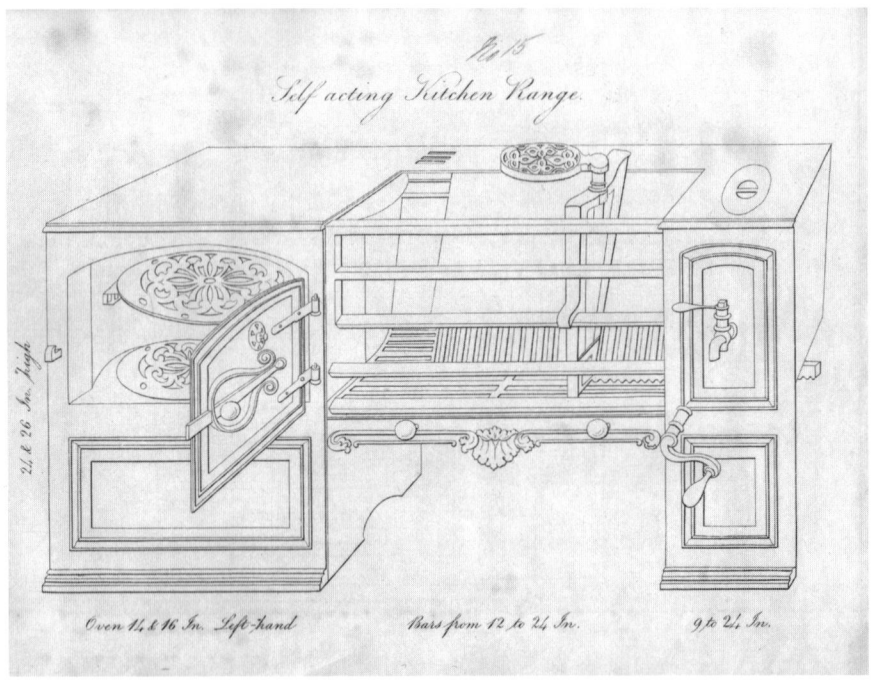

Figure 9. An open range from an undated catalogue probably dating to the 1840s of the Coalbrookdale Company, Shropshire. With its single winding cheek, this range is very similar to Robinson's model of 1780 except for the addition of a boiler on the right which extends along the back of the grate to ensure some measure of direct contact with the fire. The term 'self acting' was widely used in the trade to describe ranges which transmitted the heat directly to the oven and boiler without the assistance of flues. (The Ironbridge Gorge Museum Trust Library)

ash pit covered with a grating. Just one item was made of cast-iron – the fire-back – which protected the masonry behind the grate.

By the early to mid-eighteenth century, the majority of kitchen grates had become fixtures in the chimney opening. Small cottage grates consisted of relatively narrow front and bottom bars of wrought-iron fixed between low hobs of brick or masonry. The kitchens of larger houses were fitted with large grates ideally suited for spit roasting. They were sometimes called ranges although this name was by no means universal and throughout the eighteenth century, the term kitchen grate was also widely used.

The typical eighteenth-century range consisted of a wide grate with front and bottom bars connected to stout uprights with the two front ones often terminating in a finial. The grate was shallow from front to back but high and broad across the front so the maximum amount of radiant heat was projected for spit roasting. The grate usually incorporated two vertical side plates called cheeks with racks which engaged with pinions and a crank handle either side of the range. This enabled the cook to wind the cheeks in or outwards to adjust the width of the fire. The *Housekeeping Book of Susannah Whatman*, written in 1776, exhorts the cook to, 'keep as little fire as may be necessary, always winding up the grate after dinner'.[12] The size of the fire could also be reduced by folding down the top front fire bar. This was known as a falling bar – or fall bar – and provided a convenient resting place for utensils. Rotating circular cast-iron rings or 'swinging trivets' were usually fixed to the top of the cheeks. The trivets could support a large boiling vessel or tea kettle and swing over the fire to boil, nevertheless, large pots were still suspended over the fire on pot hangers and chimney cranes: some ranges had a crane on each side of the chimney recess. Another common feature were the sliding racks which pulled out from the front to support the spit in front of the fire. A provenanced example from Seaton Delaval Hall in Northumberland, dating to 1718–29, is held by the Castle Museum, York.[13]

After 1750, the influence of iron founders capable of producing good quality but cheap castings began to influence the development of kitchen grates. On 17 June 1751, Dr Richard Pococke (1704–65) wrote from Holyhead, 'At the ironworks here, I saw octagon ovens of cast-iron from three to four feet long and about eighteen inches diameter, to be put at the back of kitchen chimneys.'[14] As these iron ovens had their own firebox, flues and damper arrangement, they could be kept hot indefinitely and this no doubt explains the name by which they were soon known – 'perpetual' ovens. They were made in various shapes, round or arched top, octagonal, square or completely circular. Some of the oven doors were elaborately cast with decoration. The Carron Foundry, established near Falkirk in 1759, produced oven doors cast with high-quality classical reliefs in the fashionable neo-classical style: these were probably the work of the brothers James and Robert Adam, who prepared designs for the company.

Thus cast-iron enabled high-quality design to be mass produced at little cost and introduced to the kitchen. Another firm which exploited the decorative quality of cast-iron in its oven castings was the Benthall Foundry in the upper Coalbrookdale Valley in Shropshire which started business sometime in the late 1770s. In 1985 an iron oven was discovered in the derelict basement kitchen of 5 Harley Place, a large terraced house in Clifton, Bristol which was probably completed around 1815. The oven door is cast with the foundry name but also has an oval brass plate fixed to it with the name, 'Underwood & Co.' – then one of Bristol's leading furnishing ironmongers. The door is embellished with a profile bust of Admiral Howe (1726–99) taken from a Wedgwood medallion modelled by the French sculptor, John De Vaere (1755–1830) in 1798.[15] The Benthall foundry also made kitchen grates and a surviving list of their castings dating to about 1810 includes grates with 'racks, rollers and Trevets' and with either wrought or cast bars. The top bar was made either loose or falling and they could also be supplied with 'shams' which probably refers to the fixed panels at the sides. They also made 'niggards' which were false-bottom grates designed to save fuel.[16]

A large cast-iron range made at the Bucklebury foundry, east of Newbury, Berkshire in 1809 survives in situ in the kitchen of Bucklebury Manor. It is of massive proportions. The grate is five feet wide and the cast-iron hobs a further foot each bringing the overall width up to seven feet. The grate is roughly a foot deep at the top, but as the cast-iron fireback slopes forwards the grate is only about six inches deep at the bottom. There are trivets on the cheeks and cranes at each side. The date is cast on the fireback and the range also retains its smoke jack for turning the spit.

Capable of generating intense radiant heat, these large kitchen grates were primarily designed for roasting and boiling. They were not suitable for lighter cooking operations and so in large households it was usual for the range to be supplemented by a stewing stove and sometimes a

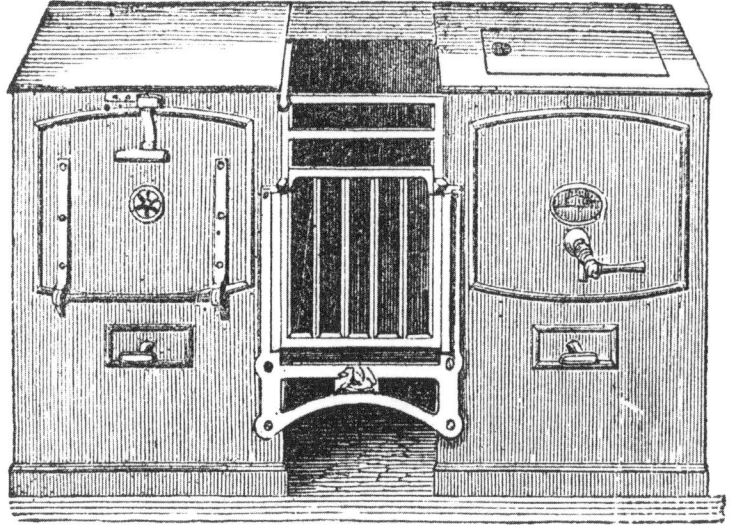

Figure 10. William Nicholson's 'Newark Cottage Range' of 1848. Hot air and smoke circulated the oven and boiler in flues which, in theory, at least, provided a more even distribution of heat to these parts. Accumulations of soot in the flues could be removed via the two small doors near the base.

Figure 11. The original range in the kitchen of Sir John Soane's house, Lincoln's Inn Fields, London. This open range, made by Thomas Deakin of Smithfield, London, was installed in 1812–3 when Soane built the house and must rank as one of the very earliest surviving kitchen ranges with an oven and boiler. A separate hot-plate is fitted in the chimney recess on the left. (Sir John Soane's Museum)

Figure 12. An open range in a cottage near Congresbury, North Somerset supplied by Harris & Kingdom, Bristol ironmongers from 1885 to 1944. When the photograph was taken in September 1996, this isolated cottage still lacked electricity and the range remained in daily use for cooking hot meals including roast dishes done in the small oven.

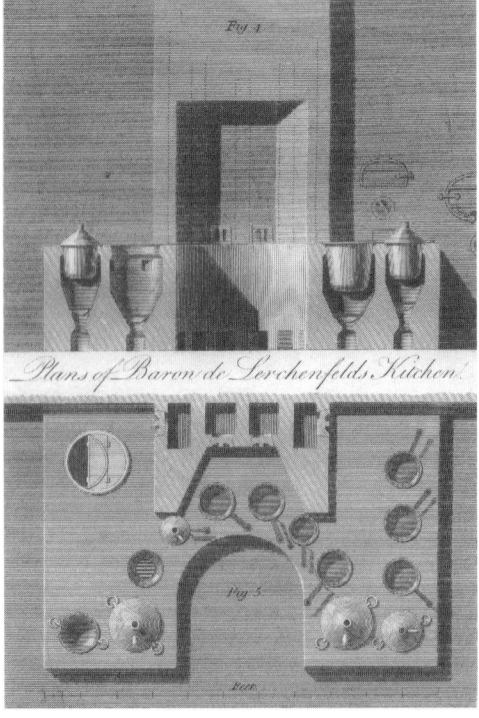

Figure 13. Plan and elevation of the brick stove designed by Count Rumford and fitted in the kitchen of the Baron de Lerchenfeld, Munich in about 1794. The various saucepans and boilers (three depicted with their low conical lids) sit in separate fireplaces or 'stoves' and each has a separate flue which conducts the smoke to the main chimney fireplace in the wall.

copper which would be used for boiling large pieces of meat, puddings and possibly the weekly wash. The stewing stove was required for the preparation of stews and sauces and had appeared in England by the seventeenth century. It usually consisted of a brick structure containing one or more small separate grates for burning charcoal. Sir John Vanbrugh's notebook for Kings Weston, Gloucestershire includes a drawing dated 1717 of a large stewing stove with three grates although by the late eighteenth century some consisted of an iron hotplate extending the width of the stove and heated by a single firebox.[17] Usually these extra facilities were placed to the side of the range along with the perpetual oven. The cooking facilities of a large eighteenth century kitchen thus presented an impressive spectacle often occupying the greater part of one wall of the kitchen with subsidiary flues from the oven, stewing stove and boiler running at an inclined angle to join the chimney throat above the range. Preparing a large meal including roast and boiled dishes, sauces and pies would have resulted, therefore, in three or four fires burning simultaneously in the kitchen generating huge quantities of smoke, heat and ash and creating a hot and unpleasant working environment – especially in warm weather.

The obvious development was to combine all these separate elements into one so that one fire could provide all the necessary heat. Iron founders appear to have started making kitchen grates combined with ovens in the 1770s. Writing of Derbyshire in 1813, John Farey wrote,

> About the year 1778, cast-iron ovens began to be made at the Griffin Foundry, now Messrs Ebenezer Smith and Company, and to be set by the sides of the grates at the public houses and some farm houses, so as to be heated by the fire in the grate when a small damper in the flue is drawn and about ten years after, square iron boilers with lids were introduced to be set at the end of a fire grate and these have spread so amazingly that there is scarce a house without these, even of cottages of the first class…[18]

The Griffin Foundry was established by John Smith, father of Ebenezer, at Brampton near Chesterfield in 1775. Soon foundries across the country were making cast-iron ranges. The earliest description of a kitchen range with a perpetual oven is contained in a patent taken out by Thomas Robinson in 1780. The oven, he claimed, was heated, 'without the Assistance of any Flew, or additional Fire' and was covered with an iron plate, 'which forms', he claimed, 'an excellent hob, and will contain sufficient heat to keep any Thing warm'.[19] He also emphasized that his range was compact. Three years later, a London iron founder, Joseph Langmead, patented a range with a boiler on the other side of the grate.[20] Thus the basic arrangement of the kitchen range incorporating an oven and boiler either side of a grate was established by 1783.

Cast-iron panels provided visual unity to the front of the range and if the range lacked a boiler then a cast-iron panel – known as a 'sham' in the trade – was substituted. The oven and boiler (or sham) were covered by cast-iron hobs which provided useful warm tops whilst the cook was able to cook over the exposed fire in-between. Toasting and broiling was done using trivets and gridirons hooked or balanced on the uppermost fire bar whilst tea kettles, pots and pans could even be placed directly on the fire. The fire, therefore, remained open to the chimney and in the nineteenth century, writers such as J.H. Walsh, Isabella Beeton and others always referred to these as 'open ranges'.

Compact and inexpensive, the open range was ideally suited to the smaller cottage, farmhouse or villa where space in the kitchen was at a premium. Such was the 'Newark Cottage Range' registered under the Act for the Protection of Articles of Utility on 12 July 1848 by William Nicholson, an agricultural implement maker of Newark-on-Trent: the following week it obtained a prize at an agricultural show in York. It was designed with a very shallow fire grate from front to back with fire-clay sides and back which protected the adjacent oven and boiler from the direct action of the fire.[21] In 1851, one of Nicholson's Newark Cottage Ranges was installed in one of four model dwellings built at Prince Albert's own expense for the Great Exhibition in Hyde Park on behalf of the Society for the Improvement of the Working Classes.[22] It was awarded a prize medal by the jurors: such ranges clearly represented a great advance on the simple cooking hearths and grates found in many cottage homes at the time.

Some range ovens, like Thomas Robinson's model, had no flues – the inner oven wall forming one side of the grate so the oven was heated by direct contact with the fire. When the range was lit, therefore, the oven was always hot. They were sometimes known as self-acting ranges as no adjustment of a damper was required. To improve the conduction of heat, some ovens were fitted with a projection of cast-iron, which conducted heat from the fire to the oven but they tended to heat unequally with

Figure 14. A typical closed range with a single oven and boiler from a Coalbrookdale catalogue of 1875. The range was available in eight widths ranging from three feet three inches to five feet. This range had no 'coving' or cast-iron panelling in the chimney recess which was left as bare brick apart from a shallow skirting above the hot-plate. (The Ironbridge Gorge Museum Trust Library)

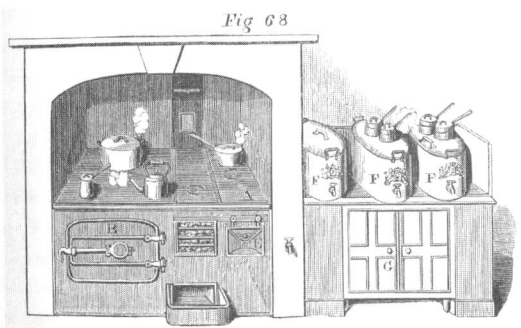

Figure 15. A closed range with oven, boiler and hot-closet from J.H. Walsh's Manual of Domestic Economy, *1857. Walsh described this as a very complete and economical stove for large families but also observed that it could not produce meat 'cooked to suit the taste of the gourmand'. Although the small grate precluded open-fire roasting, three vegetable steamers and a large steam hot-closet were provided.*

Figure 16. A convertible range from the Coalbrookdale catalogue for 1875 seen here ready for use as an open range with the cast-iron smoke canopy unfolded. Note the bright disc or 'banjo' latch which became increasingly common on ranges from the 1860s. (The Ironbridge Gorge Museum Trust Library)

the side nearest the fire being scorched while the other remained cool. Several authors of mid-nineteenth-century cookery books were far from enthusiastic about range ovens. In 1845, Eliza Acton wrote,

> They are…we should say…far from economical as regards the proportion of fuel required to heat them…The strong smell, too, emitted from the iron and diffused often, through a house, is peculiarly unpleasant.[23]

In a later edition of her cookery book, Eliza Acton said that for baking bread a brick oven was superior as there was a tendency for the surface of the loaves to become hardened and browned before the heat had reached the centre of the dough.[24] Another objection voiced by several writers was that the heating of the oven from the range required an unnecessarily large fire. In 1844, Mrs Parks wrote,

> It is commonly stated by ironmongers that ranges…with a boiler and oven perform…boiling and baking without any additional expense or consumption of fuel. This statement is absurd'[25]

But Mrs Parks was prepared to admit the sheer convenience of a range – of having constant hot water together with a hot oven – outweighed the extra expense of fuel. Some founders – perhaps in recognition of these published criticisms – continued to make oven ranges with a separate firebox.

Eliza Acton was not the first to challenge the efficiency of the range. As early as 1799, Count Rumford, the American-born soldier and scientist, roundly condemned the typical English range with these words,

> More fuel is frequently consumed in a kitchen range to boil a tea kettle than with proper management would be sufficient to cook a dinner for fifty men.[26]

Rumford advocated an entirely new type of cooking stove based on one he had tried out in the workhouse in Munich around 1790. In place of an open fireplace, he created a brickwork structure which contained up to twelve separate fireplaces which directed the heat to the underside of vessels of various shapes and sizes so that no heat was wasted. But notwithstanding Rumford's claims of huge savings on fuel, his stove was never widely adopted. He also designed an iron roasting oven which consisted of an iron cylinder with ventilation pipes. This enjoyed some limited success and critical acclaim but was not available for long.

Nevertheless, some of Rumford's principles were incorporated in a new type of range which iron founders introduced soon after the publication of his essay. This was the closed fire range which was first patented by George Bodley, an Exeter iron founder, in 1802.[27] Bodley reduced the size of the grate and covered it with an iron plate which prevented the hot draught rushing up the chimney until it had passed through flues surrounding an oven and boiler. Bodley summarized his new invention with these words,

> The meat dressed in this oven is equal if not superior to meat roasted before the fire in the common way; the cooking is attended with less trouble, and a very great saving is made in the article of fuel.

The iron cover extended across the top of the range and provided a hot-plate for stewing. Furthermore the chimney opening was sealed off which transformed the space above the range from a smoky, sooty recess into a clean, warm alcove where food could be kept warm, plates warmed and kitchen cloths dried.

Bodleys were a long-established firm of Exeter iron founders and some older people today in Devon still refer to ranges generally as 'Bodleys'. According to a later edition of Mrs Beeton, the closed range was first used in Devon for the convenience of scalding milk to make clotted cream on the hot-plate.[28] However, closed ranges are more usually associated with Leamington Spa where William Flavel (1779–1844), who had established a foundry in the town in the early 1800s, began manufacturing closed ranges under the name, 'Patent Kitcheners' in the 1820s.[29] The 'Leamington Kitchener' quickly gained acceptance. As early as 1833, J.C. Loudon (1783–1843) reported that open ranges had been, 'entirely laid aside in favour of kitcheners in villas around Leamington'.[30] Flavels won a prize for one of their ranges at the Great Exhibition in 1851 and then the Leamington Kitchener was given a further boost in 1861 when Mrs Beeton wrote, '… the improved Leamington Kitchener is said to surpass any other range in use for easy cooking by one fire'.[31]

Flavel's patent kitchener of 1830 had a roaster on one side of the fire, an oven on the other and a cistern for hot water. His advertisement in a local directory of 1830 claimed,

> The Patent Kitchener affords the most ready means of performing in the best manner either separately or at the same time, all the operations of cookery – as roasting, baking, boiling, steaming, stewing &c. with only one fire.[32]

But not everyone was convinced. Mrs Parks, for one, was inclined to reserve judgement on the closed range. 'For common English cooking and English servants', she wrote, 'we can scarcely venture to recommend dispensing with a good open fire'. She doubted if the claimed saving on fuel was actually offset by the initial high expense, and other inconveniences – such as their tendency to break down – and the necessity of frequent cleaning of the flues. Then there was the time and trouble, she said, involved in teaching a cook how to use a closed range. Nevertheless, she did concede that when the inside of the chimney was lined with white glazed tiles they had, ' a very neat and clean appearance'.[33]

Meat roasted – or 'baked' –in a range oven was held by some to be 'unwholesome and objectionable' and this well-established English prejudice against oven-roast meat persuaded some affluent householders to retain the large open range. When the Blathwayts of Dyrham Park, north of Bath, refurbished their kitchen around 1855, they opted for a traditional

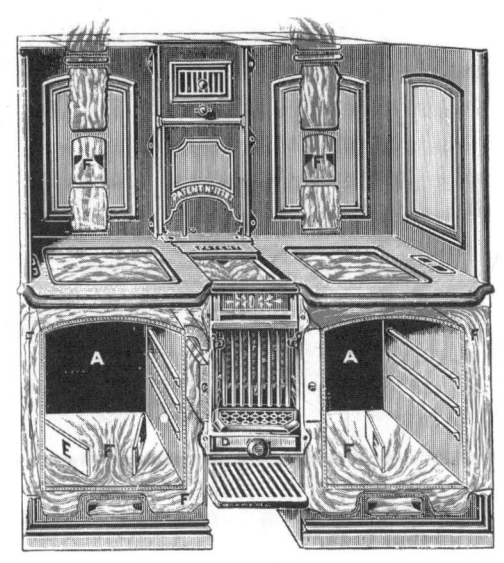

Figure 17. A very typical large range of the 1890s – the 'Swinton' – a convertible range patented by Hattersley in 1890. The range has two ovens, a back boiler and lifting fire with its characteristic vertical front fire bars. The cross-section clearly indicates the route of the hot draught around the various parts with top heat provided first to the roaster on the right.

Figure 18. The 'KB' range by Coalbrookdale, 1911. This closed range is fitted with Gibson's 'kettle-boiler fire', patented in 1909, which facilitated open-fire roasting using a bottle-jack and dangle-spit suspended from an integral crane. (The Ironbridge Gorge Museum Trust Library)

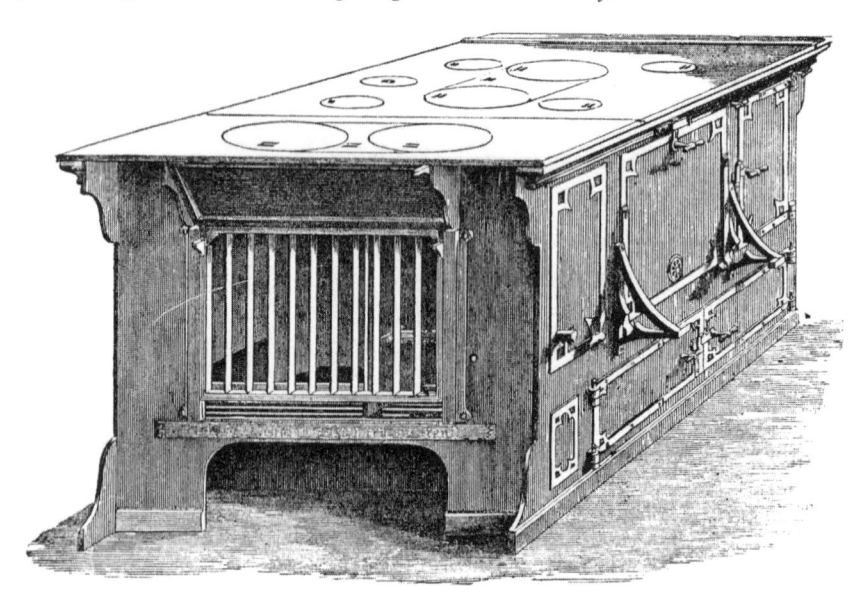

Figure 19. The 'Cosmopolitan Cooking Range' made its debut at the Great Exhibition in 1851 and aimed to combine the best features of Continental and North American cooking stoves with the English open roasting fire.

CAST-IRON PROGRESS

Figure 20. The 'Yorkshire Gas Kitchener', a combination range for coal and gas, manufactured by Beverley and Wylde of the Leeds Gas Stove Works, 1882.

Figure 21. An 'Eagle Range' with its unmistakable strap-work ornament and eagle trade mark, photographed in the derelict kitchen of 5 Harley Place, Clifton, Bristol in November 1985.

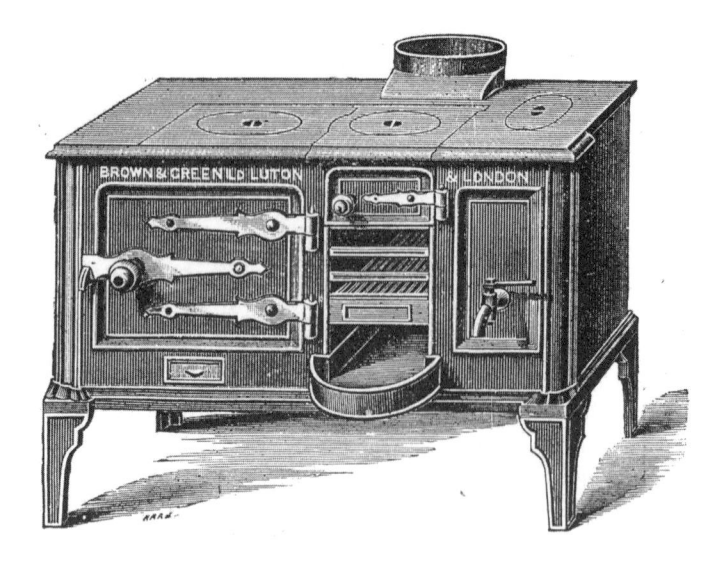

Figure 22. The 'Gem' portable range manufactured by Brown and Green, range and stove makers in Luton, 1882.

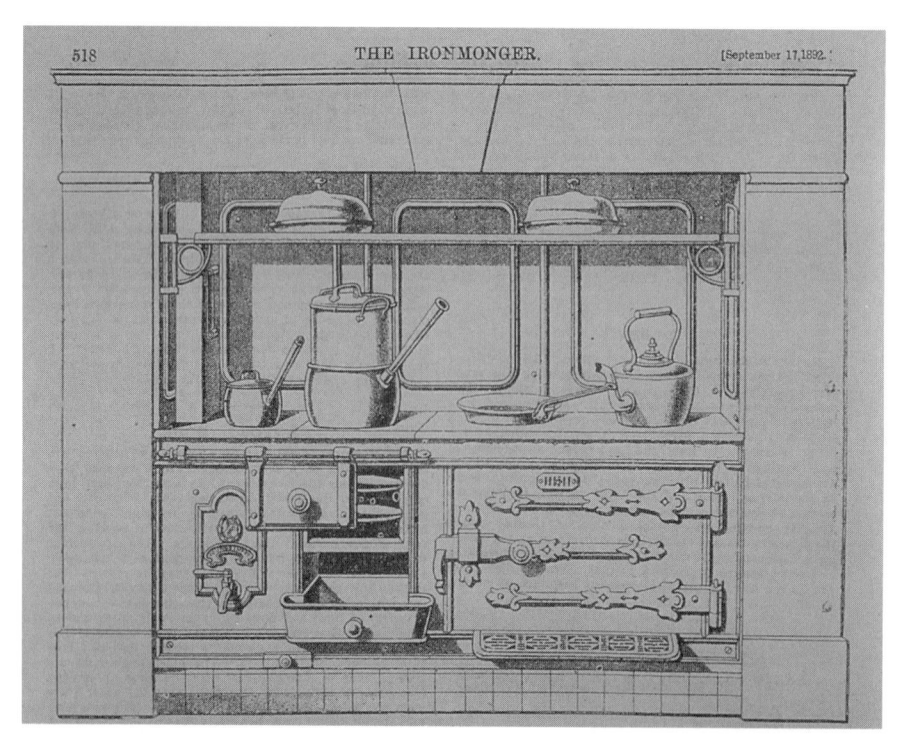

Figure 23. A closed range of 1892 made by J.D. Young & Son, iron founder and agricultural implement maker of Barnstaple, Devon.

roasting range with separate oven and stewing stove and as late as 1907 a roasting range complete with smoke jack was installed in The Skinners' Hall, London. According to J.H. Walsh in 1857, slightly further down the social scale in 'well appointed houses', an open range was often retained for the back kitchen where it served as an ancillary range – especially for open-fire roasting – when a closed range was fitted in the main kitchen.[34] As late as 1904–5, the German architect, Herman Muthesius, writing of English house design, acknowledged the importance of the open fire for two essentially English culinary specialities: roasting meat and the toasting of bread.[35] 'The English', he wrote, 'are still very fond of roasting meat at an open fire.' In the 1907 edition of Mrs Beeton, the clockwork bottle-jack for roasting meat was considered too familiar to warrant explanation. Old traditions die hard.

While the country landlords clung to their open roasting ranges, the Victorian middle classes generally adopted the closed range or kitchener. They came in all sizes – the smallest had just one oven whilst models with separate ovens for roasting and baking and fitted with a back boiler became virtually the standard in the middle-class villa in the second half of the nineteenth century. From the 1850s, as the use of fixed baths increased, ranges were required to supply hot water around the house. For this the range was fitted with a sealed wrought-iron boiler behind the grate which was fed directly from a cold water tank. Back boilers were known in the 1840s but they became more common after 1850.[36] From the 1870s most new middle-class houses were built with bathrooms and so the back boiler – increasingly supplied by mains water – was connected to a hot water storage tank or cylinder from which it circulated around the house. With so many demands being placed on the larger range, it was vital that the dampers were used correctly to direct the hot draught to where it was required, but many kitchen servants either did not appreciate this or, perhaps, simply were not prepared to bother. As *The Ironmonger* observed in 1900,

> The proper way to work a kitchener is not taught at our cookery schools and where the teacher is an average cook it is tolerably safe to say that she does not know it herself. Range makers are not over careful in issuing cards of directions with their ranges, and the result is that a large number of ranges are condemned as giving bad results simply because of wrong usage.[37]

Rather than close down the flues for the parts that were not in use, it was easier to leave them open. The result was a constant roaring fire, hotplates glowing red and unmanageably hot ovens. Then there was the unbearable heat in the kitchen and heavy fuel bills. Partly through intrinsic design faults but also through misuse, closed ranges eventually acquired the appellation, 'coal devouring monsters'.[38]

It was ironic that the closed range had been introduced to reduce the waste of fuel in open ranges when in reality it often led to heavier coal consumption. If the source of the problem was the fierce draught created by the extra flues, an obvious measure was to slow down the rate of combustion by enabling the enclosed grate to be easily converted into an open fire with direct access to the chimney. Possibly the first range to incorporate this facility was 'The Economical Derby Range' designed by Joshua Harrison, a stove-grate manufacturer of Park Street, Derby, in 1846. When the three fire doors covering the fire and a door in the chimney were opened, this closed range was turned into 'a common open fireplace'. Harrison's range was not the subject of a patent although he took out design protection according to the 1842 Act for the Protection of Articles of Utility.[39] A patent for a range which converted from a closed to an open fire was taken out by one G.H. Ellis in 1858 but it was Benjamin Wright's patent 'Lichfield Range' of 1866, manufactured by William Carter & Co. of Birmingham, which appears to have attracted more attention within the hardware trade.[40] The central part of the hotplate pulled out bodily to expose the top of the fire while a sliding door in the panelling at the back provided access to the chimney. The convertible grate was one refinement that virtually all manufacturers were to adopt. There were many detailed variations to the arrangement of sliding or hinged hotplates and of the doors or canopies which variously slid back or unfolded but by the 1890s all good-quality closed ranges incorporated some means of converting speedily from closed to open fire. The availability of an open fire in the centre of the hotplate was a boon to the traditional cook who found a useful means of broiling and toasting but the main impetus behind this improvement was achieving economy of fuel.

Improving fuel efficiency and reducing smoke emission dominated progress in fireplace and grate design in the second half of the nineteenth century and kitchen ranges were inevitably affected. An obvious measure was simply to reduce the size of the fire. In 1858, the first patent appeared

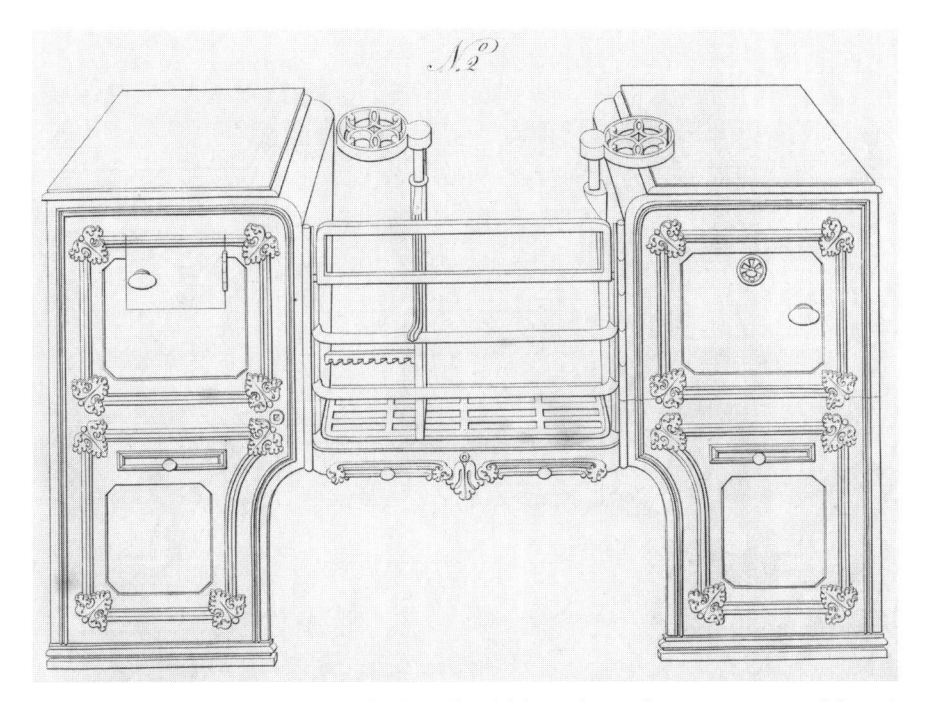

Figure 24. An open range from the undated Coalbrookdale catalogue of c.1840–50. Ranges of this style were sometimes described as Midland ranges but they were used in many parts of the country including the south and south-west. (The Ironbridge Gorge Museum Trust Library)

Figure 25. A typical north country range at an unknown location in Cumbria, photographed c.1900. (Museum of English Rural Life)

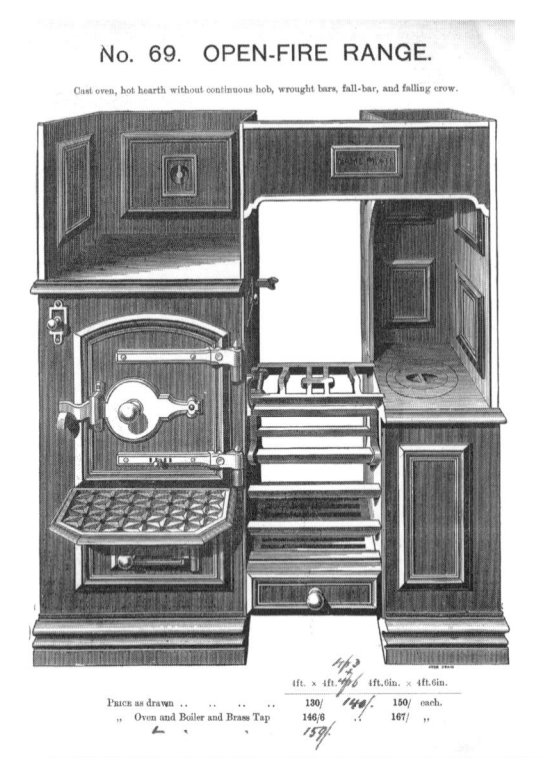

Figure 26. A 'Yorkshire' open range from the Coalbrookdale Catalogue of 1875. (The Ironbridge Gorge Museum Trust Library)

Figure 27. Kitchen at Rookhope, Stanhope, Durham, late nineteenth century. The range has the circular oven door widely found in Co. Durham and on Tyneside. (Beamish, The North of England Open Air Museum)

for a 'lifting fire' a device which raised the bottom grate to reduce the depth of the burning fuel. Like the convertible grate, the lifting fire became virtually a standard feature of late-Victorian closed ranges. The earliest involved raising the bottom grate by a rack and pinion or worm wheel but later versions, such as that fitted to the well-known 'Herald Range', made by Russells of Derby, could be adjusted with a deft flick of the foot. Less widely adopted were stoking devices designed to reduce smoke emission. The basic principle was that if fresh coals were supplied from below the fire instead of being thrown on top, the smoke would be consumed as it passed through the hot incandescent mass of burning fuel. Dr Neil Arnott (1788–1874), a leading sanitarian, introduced a smoke-consuming grate in 1854. Arnott's grate attracted much interest and two years later, William Young invented a grate made with a large revolving screw operated by a lever and ratchet which fed coal to the bottom of the fire as it turned. Thomas Radcliffe, a Leamington Spa founder, added this device to his Prize Kitchener which was awarded a medal at the 1862 International Exhibition held in London. But little was heard subsequently of this and similar devices. The success of mechanical stokers almost certainly depended upon careful management – and probably carefully selected even-sized lumps of coal – and it is doubtful that this was within the capability of the average common cook or kitchen maid.

Nevertheless, attempts to reduce smoke continued. In January 1882, ranges were exhibited at the Smoke Abatement Exhibition held in South Kensington. Here they were subject to controlled experiments to measure their efficiency and amongst those which attracted attention were the combination gas and coal ranges. The possibility of cooking by gas had been explored as early as the 1820s and 1830s but there was little real progress. Webster in 1844 had dismissed the idea as 'a novelty' although Nathan Defries, a London gas engineer was making gas cookers – along with gas baths – by the 1850s and in the same decade, Alexis Soyer, the celebrated chef at the Reform Club, promoted cooking by gas. The essential technical breakthrough came with the perfection of the atmospheric burner by Robert Wilhelm Bunsen (1811–1899) from the mid-1850s. Combined with a supply of oxygen, a gas flame was transformed into a hot blue flame capable of generating considerable heat. The production of gas cookers increased but the manufacturers encountered the usual obstacle to progress in the kitchen, the innate conservatism of the householder and especially of the cook. One solution was to combine the coal range with gas and in 1867, Messrs Hill and Wilberforce patented a range with a gas burner.[41] Beverley and Wilde of the Leeds Gas Stove Works had one on show with a gas oven and gas ring burners on top of the oven at the Smoke Abatement Exhibition. One reviewer reported that this range had been

> specially designed with the object of removing the very general objection made to cooking by gas, viz., the want of a bright, cheerful fire.[42]

The range had a gas oven and a 'boiling hearth' on top of the oven consisting of several gas ring burners. On the other side there was a boiler but in between this and the oven was the reassuring sight of the open fire of a typical Yorkshire range.

Improving flue design was another means of improving efficiency. The performance of a range was not simply a matter of its intrinsic design – or even how it was managed by the cook – but how effectively it had been set up by the bricklayer. Whilst a range gave every appearance of being made entirely of cast-iron, the reality was that behind the oven, boiler and front panels most ranges consisted largely of bricks and mortar. Some manufacturers provided directions for the bricklayer but too much depended on his ability to construct effective flues. The performance of ranges, thus, could be unpredictable: some flues simply failed to draw the hot gases evenly around the ovens. One solution was the introduction of 'self setting' ranges which were effectively free-standing units with flues contained in the body of the ironwork. Such was the highly successful 'Eagle Range', first introduced by the Eagle Range and Foundry Company of Birmingham in 1879; with its distinctive strap-work design on the oven doors, this range was enclosed in an iron casing rendering brickwork unnecessary.[43]

Self-setting ranges like the Eagle Range were still fixed in the chimney opening but towards the late nineteenth century, self-contained ranges which were free-standing – and in theory portable – became more common. The portable range broke with tradition in not being an integral part of the kitchen fireplace; instead it owed its development to portable cooking stoves which were commonly used in continental Europe and North America. Portable cooking stoves were known in the early nineteenth century: Thomas Deakin, a London ironmonger patented one as early as 1815 and in 1833, J.C. Loudon promoted the Bruges Stove which combined a small grate and oven on four spindly iron legs. It could, if required, stand in the middle of a room as the smoke was carried away by a stovepipe. Loudon considered it ideal for the cottager. In 1851, a portable range made by the leading London kitchen range manufacturer, Benham & Sons, was tried out in one of the model cottages built by Prince Albert for the Great Exhibition. It was called the Cottager's Stove and was claimed to cook a meal for twelve people using just one pound of coal or coke per hour.[44] But the portable stoves themselves were not cheap: in 1851, Benham's smallest model cost £2 10s 0d, more than double the price of the cheapest open ranges which, in the 1850s could be purchased for as little as £1 1s 0d. Nevertheless, their promoters made much of the fact that a portable range could be carried anywhere – and used anywhere – and, therefore, could be the personal property of the householder rather than a landlord's fixture. In 1858, S. & E. Ransome of London advertised the Emigrants Stove, which they claimed had been designed 'for the working classes and emigrants'.[45] If the latter found themselves temporarily homeless on the other side of the world, this stove, they claimed, could be used in the open air, even on the side of a mountain!

Larger free-standing ranges were made too – like the Cosmopolitan Cooking Range – which in 1858 cost from £16 10s 0d to £73 for the largest model. The makers, the Columbian Stove Company had one in operation at their American Stove Warehouse in Cheapside. They claimed several advantages for this range – that it was portable and required no setting in brickwork, that it was economical and also, 'as cheerful in appearance as an ordinary open fire range'. But here lay the root of customer resistance. There was no open fire for cooking or comfort and as one ironmonger's salesman conceded in 1879, there was a general dislike of the 'cribbed, cabined and confined' appearance of the American stove.[46] It was in response to this prejudice that Dobbie, Forbes & Co., introduced the Livingstone and Stanley portable ranges in 1874 which could be fitted into a conventional English fireplace. These ranges combined all the usual advantages claimed for the American stoves but they had a 'good frontage' which enabled small joints of meat, steaks, fowl and fish to be roasted or broiled in front of a visible fire. A trade advertisement of the period showed a free-standing roasting screen being used in front of one of these ranges.[47] The market for portable ranges increased during the last two decades of the nineteenth century. Several foundries in the area around Falkirk, Scotland

Figure 28. Land army girls sitting by a Cornish range in 1918. The recess to the side of the range, containing an open turf fire, was called a 'fringle'. The location is believed to be Tregavethan in Kea parish. (Royal Cornwall Museum, Truro)

Figure 29. A tin bath and bucket in front of an open range at Brierley Cottages, Sutton in Ashfield, Nottinghamshire. The photograph was almost certainly taken within a year or two of the 1953 coronation: note the picture of Queen Elizabeth on top of the television. (Courtesy of Nottinghamshire Local Studies and www.picturethe past.org.uk)

were particularly associated with this type of range. Smith & Wellstood, established in 1854 at Bonnybridge, specialized in the manufacture of American cooking stoves whilst another leading maker, Dobbie Forbes & Co., had sold 50,000 of their Larbert portable ranges by 1890.[48] Within ten years portable ranges were found in rural cottages and urban terraced housing across the country but they were also found in large kitchens where they provided a useful adjunct to the roasting range.

Whilst ranges made by large iron founders in Scotland, Yorkshire, the West Midlands and London commanded national markets, ranges were also made by many small iron foundries and distributed more locally. This resulted in a fascinating regional character to range types. Many small market town foundries primarily involved in the manufacture of agricultural implements would also usually make ranges. Across the midland counties the so-called 'Midland' range was common. Made by firms such as Brown & Green of Luton, many were made with a characteristic curved cut-away to the front panels each side of the grate below a small oven and boiler. The oven door was usually secured with an internal latch and small brass knob or drop handle whilst the front panels were usually embellished with cast decoration.

From the early nineteenth century – if not earlier – ranges in Yorkshire and other northern counties followed a different development. Whereas ranges elsewhere had the boiler and oven level with the grate, the Yorkshire range was characterized by an oven set higher than the fire. This was probably the natural consequence of setting perpetual ovens high on one side of the chimney recess. A coal burning grate – or in turf burning areas a low iron turf plate – filled the rest of the chimney space along with a low-set boiler. Above the fire a cast-iron 'sooker plate' helped draw the smoke. From these elements emerged the typical Yorkshire range made principally in Rotherham and Sheffield but also to a lesser extent in York, Leeds and Bradford.

Ranges of the Yorkshire type were widespread across much of the north of England and have been recorded as far south as Worcestershire. The ovens of Yorkshire ranges had good bottom heat and were recognized as the best for pastry and bread baking. The chief drawback with the Yorkshire range was the absence of a hotplate. Some cooks would open the oven door and use the floor of the oven as a cooking surface but it remained common for tea kettles to be suspended from hooks or 'reckons' attached to a chimney crane or 'reckon-bar' made of polished steel. From the 1860s, Yorkshire ranges were made as complete units including cast-iron panels to line the chimney recess and plate racks similar to those of closed ranges.[49] The Walker Foundry of York, for example, began the production of ranges combining a hot air oven, roasting range, hob and sooker plate with three arches entirely of cast-iron. By the mid-1860s the 'Albert' and other ranges had acquired a unity of design which was to characterize the later Yorkshire range.[50] Similar ranges were found in the north-east of England although a particular feature of ranges around Newcastle was the circular oven: these were noted in the region by Loudon as early as 1833.

Another distinctive regional type was confined to Cornwall. The Cornish range – or 'slab' – was typically a small closed range which included jambs and a canopy in cast-iron forming a fireplace surround. The slab was the cast-iron hotplate which occupied the entire width of the opening covering firebox, oven and boiler. They appeared in the second half of the nineteenth century and were made in over thirty foundries in towns across the county from Liskeard to Penzance although the chief centre of production was Redruth where the names of eight makers have been recorded.[51] Cornish ranges feature some of the most ornate cast decoration to be found on ranges anywhere in the British Isles. The side panels, canopy and oven door are often cast in high relief in various patterns including neo-classical motifs – acanthus leaves and classical figures – floral designs and the royal arms. Ranges were usually embellished further by a generous use of brass: oven door handles, makers' nameplates and edge beading around the edge of the oven door added to the overall decorative finish. The brass work was polished by proud householders until it sparkled against the soft sheen of the black leaded cast-iron. This is perfectly captured in this description of a range, recalled from a childhood spent at Portreath, near Redruth in the 1920s,

> Every kitchen in the village had at its centrepiece a massive Cornish range with its high mantle piece decorated with china dogs, cats and other ornaments. Its softly gleaming black finish and elaborate brass knobs and oven hinges reflected the rosy glow of the fire. On a cold winter night with the Atlantic gales howling round the granite cottage walls, the range with its centre of sparkling fire and singing kettle always on the hob radiated warmth and comfort. It was truly the heart of the home.

The oven doors of most Cornish ranges were secured by wrought-iron springs in the shape of a large handsome scroll. Until the mid-nineteenth century, these were common across Britain but after about 1860 were largely superseded by the ubiquitous cast-iron disc latch. The continued use of the older style of latch undoubtedly added to the overall picturesque quality of the typical Cornish range. In 1945, long before kitchen ranges had attracted much interest from historians of any kind, Noel Carrington paid tribute to the 'marvellous example of the iron and brass-founder's art' represented in the kitchen ranges of Cornish cottages in his King Penguin classic, *Popular English Art*.[52]

By the mid-1880s the range was facing serious competition from the gas companies. The price of gas halved in the second half of the nineteenth century and thanks to Bunsen's air enriched burner, from the mid-1860s gas cookers burned with a hot blue flame. Advertisements aimed to demonstrate that gas cookers could do everything the best ranges could – without the smoke and dirt, occupying less space and, if the gas companies were to be believed, at less cost. The gas companies took to hiring them out for a trifling weekly rent. By 1908 about 40 per cent of households in Bristol, for example, had turned to cooking by gas. Where gas was not available, paraffin stoves, which appeared about 1870, offered another, albeit more limited, challenge to the range. Some of the established range manufacturers such as Flavels turned from the manufacture of ranges to gas cookers whilst others, like Carron, attempted to bring the range up to date with glass oven doors and simpler external styling.

Following the First World War, the shortage of servants in middle-class households only underlined the advantages of cooking by gas. By 1920 the cleaning of the range was seen increasingly as an unnecessary chore. New houses built from the early 1920s in the rapidly expanding suburb of North Harrow by Albert Cutler, a local builder, were provided with coke boilers in the kitchen; these, he claimed, 'are rapidly superseding the old-fashioned, dirty and wasteful kitchen range'.[53] Doubtless many of the new suburbanites across the country would have shared Cutler's view of the range and welcomed its replacement for water heating. Tiled and enamelled combination grates which combined an oven, back boiler and open fireplace were fitted in some of the first generation of council houses built after 1919. But the age of the range was all but over. By the 1930s, 90 per cent of householders cooked by gas whilst a few had even progressed to cooking by electricity. The fully enclosed solid fuel cooker, the Aga, made its debut in Britain in 1929 but this Swedish invention owed nothing to the traditional British range. Kitchen ranges of all kinds continued to feature in builders' catalogues through the 1930s but increasingly their use was confined to the countryside where gas was not available. Then from the mid-1950s, strong advertising of electric cookers in some rural districts saw the demise of most of the remaining ranges.[54] By the 1960s, the range had become a museum piece – a curio. Cast-iron progress – so far as the kitchen range was concerned – had come to an end.

NOTES

1. Isabella Beeton, *The Book of Household Management* (London, 1861, and Chancellor Press, 1982), p. 32.
2. Peter Brears (ed.), *Yorkshire Probate Inventories 1542–1689,* Yorkshire Archaeological Society, 1972, vol. CXXXIV, pp. 35 and 82.
3. John S. Moore, *Frampton Cotterell & District Inventories* (Phillimore, 1976).
4. Barry Trinder and Geoff Cox, *Yeomen and Colliers* (Phillimore, 1980).
5. R. Latham and W. Mathews, *The Diary of Samuel Pepys* (Bell & Hyman, London, 1972), vol. II, p. 106, entry for 25 May 1661.
6. Pehr Kalm, *Visit to England 1748*, trans. by Joseph Lucas (Macmillan & Co., 1892), pp. 137–8.
7. David Souden (ed.), *Byng's Tours – The Journal of the Hon. John Byng 1781–1792* (Century, London, 1991), p. 69. Byng became Viscount Torrington shortly before his death.
8. David Vaisey (ed.), *The Diary of Thomas Turner 1754–1765* (Oxford University Press, Oxford, 1985), p. 38.
9. William Barnes, *Poems of Rural Life in the Dorset Dialect* (Kegan Paul, Trench Turner & Co., 1879 and 1905), p. 117.
10. P. A. S. Poole, *A Cornish Farmer's Diary* (Pool, Penzance, 1977).
11. John S. Moore, op. cit., p. 162.
12. *The Housekeeping Book of Susannah Whatman 1776–1800* (Century, 1987), p. 43.
13. Peter Brears, *The Kitchen Catalogue* (Castle Museum, York, 1979), p. 3 and p. 45.
14. J.J. Cartwright (ed.), *The Travels Through England of Dr Richard Pococke*, vol. 1, Camden Society, Second Series 42, 1888, p. 231. I am indebted to Stephen Price for this reference.
15. Robin Reilly and George Savage, *Wedgwood the Portrait Medallions* (Barrie & Jenkins, London, 1973), p. 195.
16. List of goods made at Benthall Foundry, c.1810, Shropshire Record Office, SRO 245171.
17. Sir John Vanbrugh's Designs for Kings Weston, Bristol Record Office 33746. See also Peter Brears, *The Country House Kitchen* (Sutton, 2000), pp. 100–104.
18. John Farey, *General View of the Agriculture of Derbyshire*, 1813, vol. II, pp. 19–20.
19. Robinson's range is described in a surviving advertisement sheet in the John Johnson Collection of Printed Ephemera at the Bodleian Library, Oxford. See also patent 1267, 21 October 1780.

20. Patent number 1361, 25 March 1783.
21. *Mechanics Magazine*, vol. XLIX, Saturday 22 July 1848, pp. 73–4.
22. *The Builder*, vol. IX, 1851, p. 311.
23. Eliza Acton, *Modern Cookery* (Longmans, London, 1845 and 1857), p. 561.
24. Ibid., 1857 edition, p. 595.
25. Mrs William Parks, 'On the General Arrangement of a Kitchen', in Thomas Webster, *An Encyclopaedia of Domestic Economy*, Longman Brown & Green, London, second edition, 1847, p. 815.
26. Benjamin Thompson, Count Rumford, *Essay on the Construction of Kitchen Fireplaces* (T. Cadell and W. Davies, 1799), p. 31.
27. Patent 2585, 27 February 1802.
28. Beeton, 1907 edition, p. 50.
29. *How We Build* (Sidney Flavel & Co., Leamington Spa: n.d., *c.*1937), pp. 8–15.
30. J.C. Loudon, *Cottage, Farm and Villa Architecture*, Longman, 1833, new edition, 1836, p. 1018.
31. Isabella Beeton, 1861 edition, p. 27.
32. *William West's Directory of Leamington Spa*, 1830, advertisement.
33. Parks, 1847, pp. 852–5.
34. J.H. Walsh, *A Manual of Domestic Economy* (Routledge, London), 1857, p. 154.
35. H. Muthesius, *The English House* (Berlin, 1904–5), trans. Janet Seligman (Crosby, Lockwood Staples, London, 1979), p. 97.
36. David J Eveleigh, *Bogs, Baths & Basins* (Sutton, Stroud, 2002), p. 80. Thomas Webster also referred to back boilers in 1844.
37. *The Ironmonger*, 31 March 1900, p. 612.
38. The author accepts that this name was probably given retrospectively. It is found in Lawrence Wright, *Home Fires Burning* (Routledge and Kegan Paul, London, 1964).
39. *Mechanics Magazine*, 17 October 1846, pp. 361–2.
40. Patent 1858/629 and 1866/1306.
41. Patent 1867/439. J.H. Walsh shows a gas stove attached to an open grate with a trivet made by Nathan Defries in 1857. Walsh, pp. 65–6 .
42. *Martineau & Smith's Hardware Trade Journal*, 31 January 1882.
43. *The Ironmonger*, 5 April 1879, p. 402.
44. *Journal of the Royal Agricultural Society of England*, vol. 12 1851, Royal Agricultural Advertiser, p. 24.
45. Illustrated Catalogue, S. & Ransome & Co., London, January 1858, p. 16 (Museum of English Rural Life, University of Reading).
46. *The Ironmonger*, 7 February 1879, p. 229.
47. Ibid., 1 October 1874, p. 1223 and 1 November 1874, p. 1323.
48. *Martineau & Smiths Hardware Trade Journal*, 31 January 1890, Supplement, p. 10.
49. For the development of the Yorkshire range see Peter Brears, *The Kitchen Catalogue* (York Castle Museum, 1979) and *Traditional Food in Yorkshire* (John Donald, Edinburgh, 1987).
50. Brears, ibid., pp. 4, 12 and 46.
51. John Ferguson, *Forged and Founded in Cornwall* (Cornish Hillside Publications, 2000), pp. 81–86. This contains a useful list of makers on p. 84.
52. Noel Carrington and Clarke Hutton, *Popular English Art* (Penguin, London, 1945), p. 11.
53. Dennis Edwards and Ron Pigram, *The Romance of Metro Land* (Bloomsbury Books, London, 1979 and 1986), p. 70.
54. S. Minwel Tibbott, 'Going Electric: The Changing face of the Rural Kitchen in Wales, 1945-55', *Folk Life*, volume 28, 1989–90.

OVER A RED-HOT STOVE

Figure 30. Detail from a contemporary broadside illustration of the 1714/15 London frost fair. (Author's Collection)

Figure 31. Detail from a broadside illustration of the 1683/84 London frost fair. (Courtesy of British Museum)

CHAPTER TWO

OX ROASTS — FROM FROST FAIRS TO MOPS

Ivan Day

> Here the fat Cook piles high the blazing Fire,
> And scarce the Spit can turn the Steer entire.
> Booths sudden hide the *Thames*, long Streets appear,
> And num'rous Games proclaim the crouded Fair.[1]

When John Gay composed these couplets in 1716, London had just experienced such a severe winter that the Thames froze solid for two months. The ice was so thick that it enabled a fair to be held on the river between Old London Bridge and Temple Stairs, the first so-called 'frost fair' for thirty-one years. The poet visited the scene and one of the many attractions he observed was the public roasting of an ox in front of a huge fire on the ice near Hungerford Stairs. This spectacle attracted large crowds of curious onlookers, intrigued that the intense heat of the huge fire did not melt the ice. A primitive image of the scene is depicted in a surviving broadside printed at the time as a souvenir. In the accompanying text, the fat cook of Gay's poem is identified as one 'Cripple Atkins'.[2]

There had been celebrations on the Thames when it froze over on earlier occasions; however, these rare events happened no more than two or three times in a century. Various sports and diversions took place on the river during an intense cold snap in 1309, including the building of a huge bonfire. A large feast on the ice was given to the poor by the Abbot of Reading in 1363/64, but there are no accounts of the nature of the food served. During the harsh winter of 1607/08 fires were lit on the ice to toast bread and to warm up sack.[3]

Though ox roasting may have occurred at some of these events, the earliest documentary evidence of the activity dates from the frost fair held during 'the Great Winter' of 1683/84. The name of the cook who roasted the ox at this occasion is not known, but he seems to have been a better businessman than Cripple Atkins, whose roasting activities in 1715 were open to the view of all and sundry. In contrast, the ox roasting area at the 1684 fair was surrounded by a tall wooden palisade. An opening in the high fence was guarded by a person whose role no doubt was to extract an entrance fee. Customers who paid to be let in could warm themselves at the biggest fire on the river, but if they wanted meat they probably had to fork out extra. An ox takes a long time to roast and earnings do not materialize until the end of the lengthy cooking process. By exploiting the public's sceptical curiosity about the ability of the frozen Thames to support a huge fire without melting, money could be made all day, long before the first slice was carved. As well as a number of broadsides illustrated with woodcuts and engravings of the event, a remarkable painting by Jan Griffier the Elder (c.1645–1718) clearly shows the ox roasting enclosure in the foreground. Outside its hastily erected palings, a seated woman, perhaps the cook's wife, appears to be negotiating with a fashionably dressed couple.[4]

Frost fairs were organized by the Thames watermen, whose livelihood was threatened by prolonged hard freezes. Their normal activities of ferrying Londoners and goods had to be suspended until the thaw. They considered it their right to charge a fee to anyone who wanted to stroll on the frozen river and they restricted access to the landings and steps until visitors paid up. The many attractions on the ice which they managed also provided excellent opportunities for profiteering. They built numerous sailcloth booths on the frozen river, their awnings held up by tent poles made of redundant oars. These makeshift shelters provided accommodation for temporary taverns, coffee houses, cook shops and other outlets for food and drink, usually manned by the watermen themselves. Their normal cry of 'Where shall I land thee' was replaced by 'What lack thee Sir? Beer, Ale or Brandy.' Prices were high. In one 1684 broadside about the fair, it was wryly noted,

> What you can buy for three-pence on the Shore,
> Will cost you Four-pence on the Thames or more.[5]

Another offered more detail,

OX ROASTS — FROM FROST FAIRS TO MOPS

Figure 32. Detail from a broadside of the 1683/84 London frost fair. The ox roasting enclosure is in the bottom right hand corner of the engraving. (Courtesy of British Museum)

Figure 33. Jan Griffier the Elder (c.1645–1718), The London Frost Fair of 1683/84. Oil painting on canvas. Detail showing the ox roasting enclosure. (Whereabouts unknown)

Figure 34. George Cruickshank, London Frost Fair, *etching, 1838. This detail shows a sheep being roasted at the frost fair of 1814, probably the so-called 'Lapland Mutton' mentioned in a number of accounts of the event. Note the unusual double-handled spit being turned by the cook's assistants. (Courtesy of the British Museum)*

Figure 35. Nikolaus Hogenberg (before 1500–1535), Ox being roasted in the streets of Bologna during the coronation procession of Charles V, *etching, 1530. The Latin caption translates as 'Ox stuffed with various animals'. (Courtesy of the British Museum)*

> And though I do confess they sold it dear
> There was roast Beef, and other sumptuous Cheer:
> There was both Coffee, Chocolat, and Wine
> For those that willing were to spend their Coin,
> But in this fair upon the Rock of Ice,
> All things were sold at an excessive price.[6]

The cost of a helping of roast ox at the 1684 fair varied from 6d. to a shilling, depending on the size of the slice. Prices had not changed much by the time of the last frost fair in 1814, when a slice of so-called 'Lapland Mutton', carved from a sheep roasted in front of a coal fire, was one shilling. Mutton at this time could be purchased at a butcher's shop for between 3d. and 5d. the pound.[7] Even taking into consideration the cost of fuel, which was more expensive in a hard winter, this does seem excessive.[8] Many other kinds of food could be bought from vendors on the ice. At the 1684 fair a roast beef booth which served cuts from smaller roast joints competed with the ox roasting enclosure. Other delicacies were also available,

> Hot Codlins, Pancakes, Duck, Goose, and Sack,
> Rabit, Capon, Hen, Turkey, and a wooden Jack.[9]

It would appear that some of these meats were roasted using a wooden spit-jack of some kind, perhaps another novelty spectacle aimed at pulling a crowd.[10] At the 1715 fair 'a shoulder of mutton roasted in a string' could be viewed at the 'Sign of the Rat in the Cage'. Another treat on offer was 'hot spiced gingerbread, three half peny-worth for a penny'. Not quite *buy-one-get-one-free*, but a rare bargain nonetheless. Many of the watermen's booths were set up as taverns and coffee houses and a wide range of hot beverages, ales and ardent spirits were available to the large crowds,

> And sholes of People everywhere there be,
> Just like to Herrings in the brackish Sea;
> And there the quaking Water men will stand ye:
> Kind Master, drink you Beer, or Ale, or Brandy:
> Walk in, kind Sir, this Booth it is the chief,
> And what you please to Eat or Drink, 'tis here,
> No Booth, like mine affords such dainty cheer.
> Another crys, Here Master, they but scoff ye,
> Here is a Dish of famous new-made Coffee.[11]

Just like their terrestrial equivalents, these improvised taverns and other watering holes on the ice displayed inn signs. At the 1684 fair, most had fairly orthodox names like the Three Tuns, the Duke of York's Coffee House and the Horn Tavern. Some had less delicate designations,

> Where e'ry Booth hath such a cunning Sign,
> As seldome hath been seen in former time;
> The *Flying Piss-pot* is one of the same,
> The *Whip and Egg-shell*, and the Broom by name:
> And there if you have Money for to spend,
> Each cunning Snap will seem to be your Friend.[12]

The Whip and Egg Shell served tea and chocolate, but what delicates were offered by the snaps (swindlers) at the Flying Piss-pot are not disclosed.[13] Hot spiced ale and mum were available from other booths. Gin creeps into the proceedings during the course of the eighteenth century. In 1715, one tent was set up as a Geneva Booth. During the fairs of 1739 and 1814 gin and gingerbread were frequently sold together,

> Some Soldiers shivering in their red
> Attack the Gin and Gingerbread[14]

Gin in particular was consumed in vast quantities. A satirical print by George Cruikshank of the 1814 fair shows a makeshift canvas inn displaying a sign inscribed 'Gin and Gingerbread sold here wholesale'.[15] By this time, although gin was ubiquitous, some of the other drinks sold by the taverns had changed. A slice of roast beef or a mutton pie could be washed down with a glass of Old Tom, or 'Fine purl, good gin and rum', sold at the City of Moscow tavern and other 'fuddling tents'. Purl was a speciality of the watermen. Originally it was hot ale flavoured with wormwood and spices, but there was also 'purl royal' for those who could afford it, a kind of wormwood wine. Purl was customarily consumed as a piping hot draught in the early morning by watermen and colliers, but it was also an ideal drink for warming chilled bones at a frost fair. According to Mayhew it was still being served steaming-hot from purl boats moored on the river in the middle of the nineteenth century, though by this time it usually consisted of a mug of ale fortified with gin.[16]

Figure 36. Detail from printed broadside, 1814, by J. Pitts of Seven Dials. (Courtesy of the British Museum)

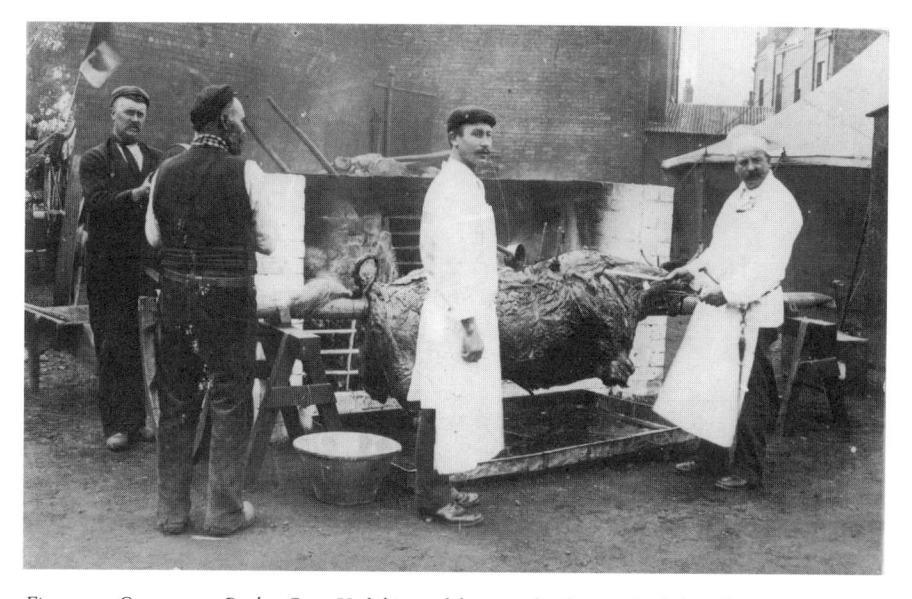

Figure 37. Ox roast at Batley Carr, Yorkshire, celebrating the diamond jubilee of Queen Victoria in 1897. (Author's collection)

Figure 38. Plate used at Batley Carr Ox Roast, June 26 1897. Porcelain, W. Adams and Co., Tunstall. Diameter, 206 mm. (Author's collection)

Figure 39. Plate used at an 1885 ox roast to celebrate the royal assent for the Manchester Ship Canal Bill, the brainchild of the engineer Daniel Adamson (1820-90). The Bill gave the go-ahead to the scheme to build a canal to link Manchester with the sea. This was welcomed by communities in the Manchester area, such as Eccles and Patricroft, as a promise of future prosperity. Porcelain, S. Radford, Fenton. Diameter, 260 mm.

A frost fair was not a good time to be of a bovine persuasion. While one ox rotated on a spit, another was usually being baited by dogs on the ice nearby,

> And on the River near our Royal Court
> The Bull was baited, making famous Sport:
> The raging Bull the nimble Dogs he Scorns,
> And in his Fury tost them with his Horns,
> An Oxe was roasted with the Horns and all,
> Near to the most renowned Court White-Hall;
> Upon the Ice, and clear from any Shore,
> The like was ne're seen in any Age before.[17]

These two events were not really linked. The animal that ended up on the spit was an ox, a castrated bull, while that tormented 'for sport' was a fully intact and extremely annoyed bull. Nevertheless, in other parts of the country there were strong associations between bull baiting and feasting on beef. After the notorious Stamford Bull Running, an annual custom formerly held in the Lincolnshire town on 13 November, the bull was slaughtered and fed to the poor at a bargain price. A letter to the antiquarian William Hone from Joseph Jibb of Sleaford on October 17 1825 was freshly penned just a few days after the Bull Running of that year. Following a detailed account of the indignities suffered by the poor creature, Jibb concludes his letter thus,

> the amusement continues until night puts a stop to the proceedings; the baited animal is then slaughtered, and his carcass sold at a reduced price to the lower classes, who to 'top the day,' regale themselves with a supper of bull beef.[18]

After a similar event held in Tutbury on the Derbyshire-Staffordshire border, the bull was fattened up and fed to the poor at Hardwick Hall for Christmas.[19] There were other festivals and fairs at which animals were slaughtered and then roasted for the benefit of the poor. One of these, a ram roasting fair, survives to this day at the Devon village of Kingsteignton. It formerly took place on Whit Tuesday, but has now been moved to Spring Bank Holiday Monday. A visitor to the fair in 1883 recorded his impressions,

> A lamb is drawn about the parish on Whitsun Monday in a cart covered with garlands of lilac, laburnum, and other flowers, when persons are requested to give something towards the animal and attendant expenses; on Tuesday it is killed and roasted whole in the middle of the village…The lamb is then sold in slices to the poor at a cheap rate.[20]

It is tempting to think that this was a survivor of some ancient ritual sacrifice. Local legend states that the custom dates back to a remote period before Christianity when a drought was afflicting the village. A ram was sacrificed and a new stream miraculously appeared. However, there are no reliable records of the event occurring earlier than the nineteenth century.[21]

There were ram roasts in other parts of Devon. One in the village of Holne was held on May Day morning; another, at nearby Buckland-in-the-Moor, on Midsummer's Day. Just like Kingsteignton, both these events involved the ritual slaughter of a ram. In 1853 a Devon parson gave a very detailed account from personal memory of the Holne affair, which he recollected as being a very sanguinary event,

> at the village of Holne, situated on one of the spurs of Dartmoor, is a field of about two acres, the property of the parish, and called the Ploy Field. In the centre of this field stands a granite pillar (Menhir) six or seven feet high. On May morning before daybreak, the young men of the village used to assemble there, and then proceed to the moor, where they selected a ram lamb, and, after running it down, brought it in triumph to the Ploy Field, fastened it to the pillar, cut its throat, and then roasted it whole, skin, wool, etc. At midday a struggle took place, at the risk of cut hands, for a slice, it being supposed to confer luck for the ensuing year on the fortunate devourer. As an act of gallantry the young men sometimes fought their way through the crowd to get a slice for the chosen among the young women, all of whom, in their best dresses, attended the Ram Feast, as it was called. Dancing, wrestling, and other games, assisted by copious libations of cider during the afternoon, prolonged the festivity till midnight.[22]

The Victorian ethnologist Sir Laurence Gomme used this gripping account to construct a complex theory of sacrifice, arguing that the Holne ram roast and others like it were indeed relics of pagan ritual feasts. However, four years after Gomme's book was published, the local parson's memoirs of the event were strongly disputed by a Devon historian, who claimed that the Holne ram feast had never been the bloodthirsty occasion suggested.[23] More recent researchers have also been sceptical. In 1950, the folklorist Theodora Brown visited the Kingsteignton ram roasting and recorded her impressions in a brief note. She reported that the local butchers who organized the affair had no idea of its origins. As to the Holne ram roast, with its connections to ancient blood-lettings at the local menhir, she wryly commented, 'alas, in the way of such matters, the truth has never caught up with the more exciting fiction, and the bloody rites of Holne are eagerly cited over and over again.'[24]

What is common to all these events is the emphasis on charity. Slices of the roasted animal were sold to the poor of the parish at a reduced price. This is in marked contrast to the blatant profiteering of London frost fair ox roasts, which were run as purely commercial enterprises. However, it is possible that even these had their origins in feasts for the poor, like that given by the Abbot of Reading on the frozen Thames during the harsh winter of 1363/64.

An ox was regularly donated at Christmas-time to the poor of the Durham village of Houghton-le-Spring by Bernard Gilpin (1517–83), the rector of the local church. Gilpin was archdeacon of Durham Cathedral and became rector of the parish church of St Michael and All Angels in 1557. In a biography written by his descendant William Gilpin, it is related that,

> Every Thursday throughout the year a very large quantity of meat was dressed wholly for the poor; and every day they had what quantity of broth they wanted. Twenty-four of the poorest were his constant pensioners. Four times in the year a dinner was provided for them, when they received from his steward a certain quantity of corn, and a sum of money; and at Christmas they always had an ox divided among them.[25]

In addition to this Christmas offering, other oxen were cooked at Michaelmas, at the time of an ancient local fair known as the Houghton Feast. Even when Gilpin was short of stock from his own fields, he endeavoured always to provide cattle at this time of year. In a letter to an associate he complained of a shortage, 'Where I have had against Michaelmas six or seven fat oxen, and five or six fat cows, I have now neither cow nor ox,

Figure 40. Ox paraded on a cart on its way to being roasted in the town of Patricroft to celebrate the passing of the Manchester Ship Canal Bill in 1885. (Courtesy of Salford Library)

but must seek all from the shambles.'[26] The Houghton Feast was revived in 1967 by the local Rotary Club.

One fair in particular had very strong religious links to oxen, though there is no surviving evidence to suggest that ox roasts formed part of the celebrations. This was the horn fair at Charlton on the north side of Blackheath in south London, which was held on St Luke's Day, 18 October. Revellers wore gilded horns on their heads to the fair, a practice first recorded in 1598. According to the antiquarian William Hone,

> the horn bearing may be conjectured to have originated from the symbol, accompanying the figure of St. Luke: when he is represented by sculpture and painting, he is usually in the act of writing, with an ox or cow by his side, whose horns are conspicuous. These seem to have been seized by the former inhabitants of Charlton on the day of the feast's festival, as a lively mode of sounding forth their rude pleasure for the holiday.[27]

If the Charlton fair had religious origins these were soon overlooked or forgotten, as the horn-bearing custom eventually degenerated into a raucous affair associated with cuckolding. Daniel Defoe visited the fair, and described it as 'a rabble of mad-people, at Horn-Fair; the rudeness of which I cannot but think, is such as ought to be suppressed, and indeed in a civiliz'd well govern'd nation, it may well be said to be unsufferable.'[28]

Figure 41. The Oldham miners' strike medallion of 1858. Tin alloy; diameter 31.5mm.
Left. Obverse: Representation of an ox standing facing left in centre of field surrounded by the legend 'The Labourer Is Worthy Of His Hire'. Below in four lines the legend, 'Roasted Whole / Oldham / Nov. 22nd / 1858'.
Right. Reverse: This side bears the legend in eight lines 'In / Commemoration / Of The / Feast To The Colliers / Given As A Mark Of Public / Sympathy & Respect / For Their Conduct On / Strike'.

In 1785 the antiquarian and lexicographer Francis Grose described the fair in similar terms,

> It consists of a riotous mob, who after a printed summons dispersed through the adjacent towns, meet at Cuckold's Point, near Deptford, and march from thence in procession, through that town and Greenwich, to Charlton, with horns of different kinds upon their heads; and at the fair there are sold rams horns, and every sort of toy made of horn; even the gingerbread figures have horns.[29]

Some relics of the original religious nature of the horn fair endured – it was customary for the crowd to process three times round the church, where a sermon was preached – until the closing decades of the eighteenth century.[30] Although it is recorded that the standard food and drink outlets were set up in booths at Charlton horn fair, there is no mention of the roasting of oxen or other animals. However, at a similar horn fair held in the small village of Ebernoe near Petworth in Sussex, a ram is roasted and its horns presented to the winning team of a cricket match which takes place as the animal is cooked. It is claimed that the custom is of great antiquity, but died out and was revived in 1864. However, there are no surviving records of its occurrence before this date.[31]

It would be tempting to think that ox and ram roasts had their origins in ancient sacrificial rites, but the truth is probably much more prosaic. Roasting a whole animal provided a sizeable amount of food and was ideal for large-scale charitable feasts and gatherings like fairs. Some hiring fairs or 'mops', particularly those in the Midlands, were famous for their ox roasts, the height of their popularity occurring in the nineteenth century; some were still going strong in the early twentieth. In 1915, the local folklorist L. M. Stanton explained that,

> In the district of Shipston-on-Stour, the Hiring Fairs took place in the autumn; that at Shipston on the first Saturday before Old Michaelmas Day; Stowe-on-the-Wold the first Thursday before, and that at Chipping Norton the first Wednesday before. There were three Mops, or hiring fairs, at intervals of a week, the third being called the Run-away Mop, where men and maids who had run away from places taken at the first Mop might be hired. If they ran away after that they might be put in prison by their masters. Besides these hiring fairs in Stratford, Shipston, and other places there was also a Michaelmas fair, the Bull-roast; this is still kept up, and an ox roasted whole in the street.[32]

A local newspaper account from 1907 explained how the preparations for the Bull-roast in Stratford-upon-Avon started at a very early hour,

> And now to the principal feature of the Fair – the roast. Six oxen and about a dozen porkers were spitted, and close upon 6.30am the proceedings commenced, being watched with great interest throughout the morning by townspeople and visitors. Some had their doubts as to whether the caterers had not provided a little too bountifully for the occasion, but their fears in this direction were soon dispelled, for by midday the ribs of the majority of animals were laid bare.[33]

As well as providing a treat for fair-goers, whether on the frozen Thames or at *terra firma* mops, the roasting of oxen was also a central event in the celebration of national events such as coronations, jubilees, key acts of parliament, marriages and coming-of-age festivities. This was also the case in some other countries. In 1530, for instance, the citizens of Bologna were regaled with a roast ox when Charles V was crowned in the city as Holy Roman Emperor.

In Britain, some very detailed accounts of ox roasts connected to a royal event are given in a small book published anonymously in 1809, the year of George III's golden jubilee.[34] On the day of the jubilee (25 October), oxen and sheep were roasted in hundreds of towns and villages all over the country. Although these occasions were enjoyed by all, they were organized for the benefit of the poor. The authoress gives accounts of the jubilee entertainments held in just about every borough in Britain. A typical entry is this one for Fawley in Hampshire,

> Andrew Berkeley Drummond, Esq., gave a fat ox, (above forty score weight), to the poor of the parish, which was roasted whole, on an eligible spot on Ash Down. It was roasted by two o' clock in the afternoon of the 25th, when it was cut out and divided amongst the poor, at tables placed on the Down for the purpose, with 100 gallon loaves, and six hogsheads of good strong beer, raised by a subscription from the gentlemen of the neighbourhood.[35]

Not surprisingly, the most lavish ox roast took place at Windsor, where a huge triumphal arch designed by James Wyatt, decorated with allegorical paintings and thousands of lanterns, stretched from the Town Hall to the Castle Inn. In the words of the authoress,

> At one o' clock, the Queen, Princess Elizabeth, the Dukes of York, Kent, Cumberland, and Sussex, attended by Lady Ilchester, Lord St. Helen's, the Mayor and Corporation of Windsor, with white wands, and others, walked to the Batchelor's Acre for the purpose of seeing the ox roasted whole, her Majesty leaning on the Duke of York's arm… Fifty Batchelors were ready, at the outside of the gate, which opens to the Acre: and when the royal party descended from the stand, guarded them at the fire-place, where the ox was roasting; they then proceeded to view the construction of the grates and walls for roasting the ox, which were so well contrived as to roast two whole sheep at the same time, and then returned to the booth. The butchers employed in managing the cooking of the whole animals, were dressed upon the occasion in blue frocks and silk stockings: they cut the first prime pieces from the ox and sheep, and put them upon silver plates, and the bachelors and butchers waited upon the royal party with them. They all tasted and appeared highly pleased with the novelty.[36]

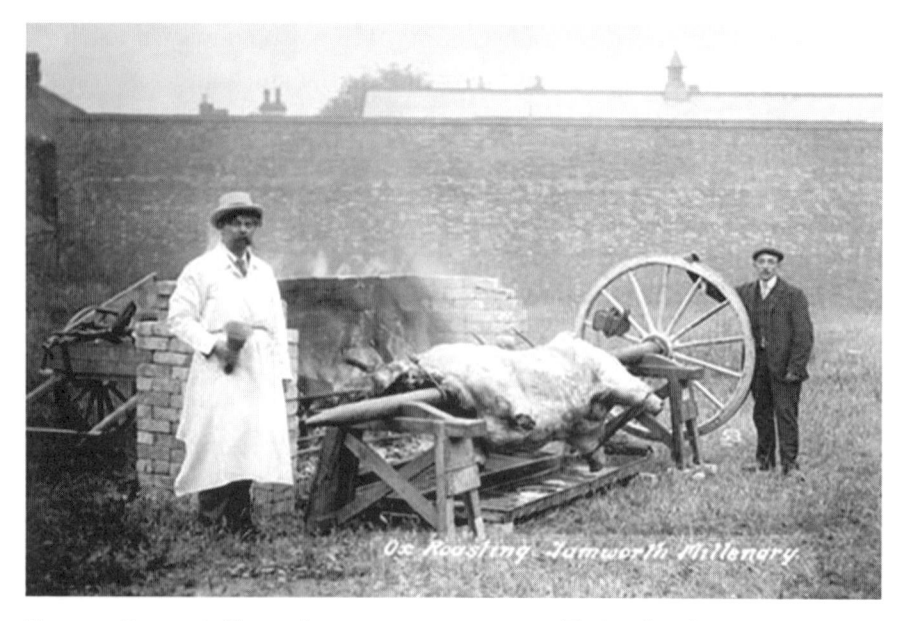

Figure 42. Ox roast in Tamworth at a town pageant in 1913. The hearth and spit arrangements are identical to those illustrated in the seventeenth-century frost fair broadsides. Note the balancing weight on the wheel. (Author's collection)

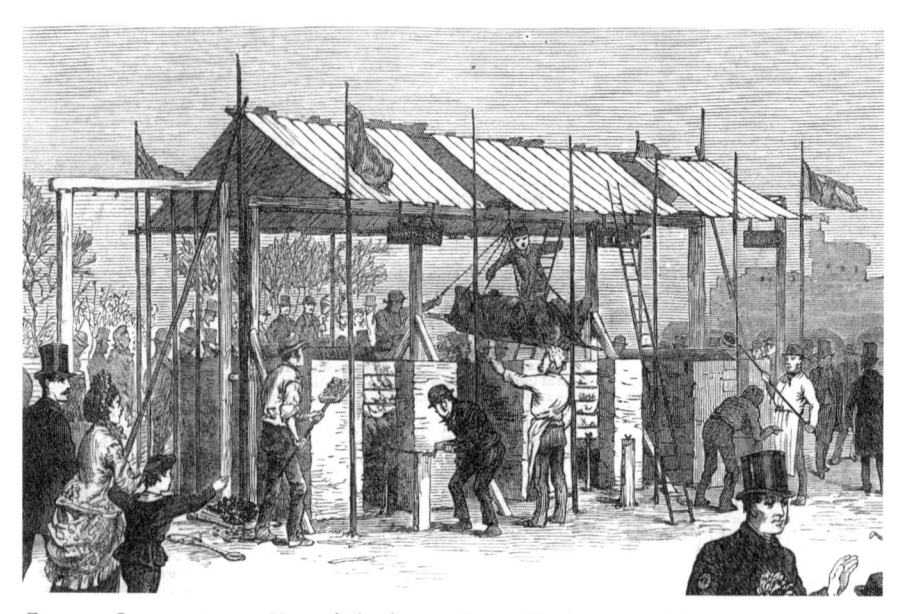

Figure 43. Oxen roasting at a Hospital Thanksgiving Day at Windsor in 1872. The spits are not furnished with the usual wheels. It is possible that the same system is being used as that illustrated in figure 34, with two men at either end of the spit.

One of the Canons of St George's Chapel delivered a sermon after the event, the text of which gives some interesting clues to the culture of patriotism and loyalty which underpinned proceedings of this kind.

The chief purpose of this address was to impress upon the minds of the hearers a religious sense of the mercies of Providence, in granting to this country, in the midst of the desolation of Europe, that permanence and due balance of the different parts of our happy constitution, under which all ranks enjoyed the highest degree of liberty compatible with order, and everyone was secure in his person, his property, and every mode of increasing it.[37]

At a time when Europe had been set on fire by Bonaparte, every Englishman, no matter what his rank, could celebrate the endurance and stability of their nation with bumpers of ale and generous helpings of roast ox. With these sentiments on beef and liberty ringing in their ears, the royal party returned to Batchelor's Acre for second helpings of beef and plum pudding. Though this particular ox roast was graced with a visit by the royal family, its real aim was to feed the Windsor poor. It was paid for chiefly by the Prince of Wales and his brothers and sisters. This pattern of patronage by the rich for the benefit of the less well-off was repeated up and down the country. At nearby Reading, the Master Butchers contributed a fine fat ox and three barrels of strong beer, while the Master Bakers distributed 'a proportionate quantity of bread to the surrounding populace, who greeted this act of liberality with loud cheers of acclamation'.[38] Plum puddings were also made for these events and were usually served before the meat. An ox roasted at Garnons in Herefordshire was stuffed with a bushel of potatoes.[39]

Even the exiled Louis XVIII, then living at Hartwell House in Buckinghamshire, donated £100 to pay for a feast for the poor of the village. Prisoners in gaols up and down the country also enjoyed beef and plum pudding dinners paid for by subscription. Deserters were pardoned and prisoners of war repatriated, all being sent on their way with a beef dinner. Tenants were frequently waited upon at table by their landlords, who afterwards went to their own private entertainments, where they dined in the sophisticated style to which they were accustomed. The jubilee was an occasion when the stout hearts of England, whatever their rank, were at one in patriotic pride. The cement that bonded them together was roast ox, plum pudding and strong beer.

Most ox roasts were started a day in advance. To get the fire up to the correct temperature it was usually allowed to burn for six hours or so before the ox was put down. Cooking times varied according to the size of the carcass and the nature of the fuel used, but it could take anything between twelve and twenty-six hours. An account of the 1809 Chester jubilee ox roast gives some very useful details about how these events proceeded,

> An ox, the gift of John Egerton, Esq. of Oulton Park, which had been slaughtered for the purpose of roasting whole, was paraded on the preceding evening being ready spitted, with horns and tail gilt, decorated with ribbons and attended by a band of music, with the colours of the several clubs of the city. Behind the ox, on the same carriage, rode the butcher, with knife drawn; thus the procession proceeded to Power Field, near the walls of the city, where a building was erected for the purpose of roasting. The fire was lighted at two, and the ox put down at eight on the Tuesday evening; by twelve o'clock the next day it was as well and as regularly roasted as any joint of meat could have been done by the most experienced cook.[40]

Though the ox's skull was normally removed, its horns and tail were always kept intact. This procession with its gay ribbons and gilt horns is reminiscent of the floral decorations and parading of the ram at Kingsteignton. However, it is obvious that the Chester event was merely a case of early-nineteenth-century civic pageantry, rather than a relic of pre-Christian ritual sacrifice. The Kingsteignton ram roast was first described in 1883 (seventy-four years after the Chester ox roast) and it is likely that this episode too was rooted in some similar display of local pageantry. Armed with their copies of Frazer's *Golden Bough*, the over-enthusiastic folklorists of the late Victorian period were only too keen to invest our national traditions with more arcane significance than they probably deserve.

The little book about George III's jubilee celebrations was republished in 1887 – the year of Queen Victoria's jubilee. There were very few people alive who could recollect the great feasts and ox roasts of 1809, so the re-issue was a reminder to the nation of the entertainments appropriate for such an event. An introductory poem by the publisher's wife stated its aims,

> Nearly eighty years now since the King's jubilee.
> But England to-day, far more great, far more free,

OX ROASTS — FROM FROST FAIRS TO MOPS

Figure 44. Postcard of a bullock being roasted at an early twentieth century mop fair in Stratford-upon-Avon. A large weight has been lashed to the wheel to balance the spit. (Author's collection)

Figure 45. Postcard of an early twentieth-century mop fair ox roast in Stratford-upon-Avon. Note the U-shaped skewers used to secure the ox to the spit. (Author's collection)

Figure 46. A postcard illustration of an early twentieth-century mop fair pig roast in Stratford-upon-Avon. (Author's collection)

Figure 47. Detail of a postcard illustration of two butchers carving a roast ox at an early twentieth-century Stratford-upon-Avon mop fair. (Author's collection)

Calls her sons and her daughters afar and anear,
To join her in keeping this Jubilee year.[41]

The nation needed no such encouragement; patriotic ox roasts were once again held with enthusiasm all over the country. Likewise, ten years later in 1897, Victoria's diamond jubilee was celebrated nationwide with similar events. Just like the ox roasts of 1809, their Victorian equivalents were organized by committees and funded by public subscription.

Ox roasts were held to mark other important occasions. In 1776, the Duke of Bridgewater treated 600 workmen to a feast of roasted ox to celebrate the completion of the Runcorn Canal.[42] This tradition continued right through the nineteenth century and ox roasts were often held when major civil engineering projects were given royal assent. As the Industrial Revolution unfolded, its great achievements were regularly celebrated with heroic feasts of roast ox and plum pudding. Dedicatory medals were struck, ceremonial carving knives commissioned and serving plates transfer-printed with appropriate designs.

Not all ox roasts were establishment affairs and some were tinged with the clear voice of dissent. One of these, perhaps the most extraordinary of the Victorian industrial period, was that held in Oldham as a benefit for the local colliers during a bitter strike in 1858. The strike was a response to the mine owners' plans to reduce the men's wages. Despite a great deal of hardship the colliers held out for twenty weeks, and were eventually victorious. A week before the strike ended subscriptions were collected, and local supporters treated the men to an ox feast. The beast, which weighed in at more than 12 cwt, was described as 'a gradely fat un' and was bought in from Dunham Park for £21. Roasting commenced at 2.30 a.m. The first slices of meat were cut from the animal at 1.00 p.m. However, some of these were apparently still a little raw and were placed in the dripping-pan, so the radiant heat from the enormous fire could finish off the job. One hundred plum puddings, each weighing 5 lb, were also made for the occasion. After a parade around the town headed by a brass band and with a banner inscribed 'The Labourer is Worthy of his Hire', 642 miners sat down to dine at about 2.30 p.m. Knives engraved with the same legend were given to each man to cut his meat. The meal started with generous helpings of plum pudding, followed by beer, bread and beef. When the men had eaten their fill, 300 wives and children sat down

Figure 48. A three-hundredweight baron of beef and sixty fowls roasting in the London Guildhall kitchen for Lord Mayor's Day. The range was sixteen feet across and seven feet high. It took a ton of coal to roast each of the two barons. Although the birds are being turned by a smoke-jack, the great baron is being rotated by hand. The cook on the platform on the left is turning a handle which is attached to a simple gear system behind the chimney breast. The gigantic spit was borrowed from the Guildhall in 1820 to roast an ox at Camden Place for the coming of age of the Marquis of Camden's eldest son. Steel engraving from the The Illustrated London News, *13 Nov. 1887.*

Figure 49. The bringing-in of the baron. The baron of beef is decorated with flowers and emblazoned with the Arms of the City of London and two Union flags. Steel engraving from The Illustrated London News. *13 Nov. 1887.*

for their share. None of the engraved knives used at the event appears to have survived, but a remarkable commemorative medal has recently been discovered by Mark Smith.[43]

In the second half of the nineteenth and early twentieth century many ox roasting events were photographed. Postcards of these images were sold to visitors at mop fairs and other roasting events in much the same way as were the souvenir broadsides in earlier times. Comparison between early broadside images of ox roasts and Victorian photographs show that equipment and techniques changed very little over the centuries. A large roasting hearth was usually improvised out of brickwork, but because of its temporary nature no mortar was used to consolidate the joints. Large cob-irons set at an angle against a sloping hearth are shown in a woodcut of 1684. This is probably an artistic error, because a 6 to 7 cwt ox would need much more support than these could afford. Nineteenth-century ox-roasting hearths usually had very large fire baskets made from long iron bars. It is likely that earlier ones had large wrought-iron fire dogs for supporting wooden logs. At an ox roast in Windsor in 1872 in aid of the Foundling Hospital, three back-to-back roasting hearths were constructed under a purpose built shelter and the oxen lowered in by block and tackle. There were two access corridors between the hearths to facilitate feeding the fires with coal or coke.

From the very earliest times ox roasts were customarily organized by butchers. They not only slaughtered the animal, but also had the skill needed to attach their massive carcasses securely to the spit. According to a contemporary account, the ox roasted at the 1715 frost fair was knocked down by a butcher called Mr Hodgson, who claimed it as an ancestral right. His father had knocked down the ox roasted at the 1684 frost fair and he himself went on to provide them for the fairs of 1715/16 and 1738/9.[44] Butchers were always key members of the ox roast committees that took charge of these events, though they were often joined by the local bakers who provided bread for the occasions. It was the butchers who tended to the roasting of the animal, often in shifts through the night. They also carved and served the meat. Professional cooks were rarely involved.

A long, sturdy spit, always round in section, was pushed through the ox underneath its spine. The spit was supported on substantial wooden trestles at either end and rotated by means of a large wheel, which enabled the animal to be turned with ease, even by one man, though two spit turners on either side are often shown. Sometimes a heavy weight was tied on the side of the wheel that corresponded to the animal's spine. This served to balance the spit and made it easier to turn.

None of the early woodcuts show how the ox carcass was secured to the spit, but nineteenth- and early twentieth-century photographs depict skewer arrangements probably very similar to those used in earlier times. Three or more large skewers shaped like giant fencing staples were usually employed to force the animal's spine against the spit shaft (figs. 45 and 47). These were sometimes threaded and tightened with nuts. A large dripping-pan, or sometimes a number of smaller ones, was placed underneath to catch the melting fat and gravy. Large ladles with very long handles were used periodically to baste the roasting animal, extra fat being kept in reserve in a large pancheon or bowl. Unlike modern so-called 'hog-roasts', where whole pigs are rotated over large pans of smouldering charcoal or gas flames, oxen were always roasted in front of the fire for maximum succulence and flavour.[45]

The folk pageantry attendant on ox roasting, such as the parading of an often decorated animal, and the ritual carving of the first slice, may have influenced the way in which our national dish was served at more elevated occasions. The barons of beef enjoyed at state occasions such as the Lord Mayor's Banquet, were usually ornamented with patriotic motifs and paraded solemnly around the hall. At a jubilee celebration in Norwich in 1806, a 172 lb roasted baron surmounted with the Union flag was carried into St Andrew's Hall by four grenadiers to the sound of fifes and drums. It was carried twice round the hall then placed under a painting of Lord Nelson and surrounded with patriotic emblems.[46]

At the annual feast on Lord Mayor's Day, two giant barons of beef, each weighing three hundredweight, once used to be served to more than a thousand diners. The barons were roasted the day before the feast and allowed to cool. The next morning they were paraded in to the hall by the cooks as part of a pageant known as 'the bringing in of the baron of beef'. A newspaper report of the preparations for the Mayor's feast of 1847 describes the ceremony,

> a procession was formed from the Kitchen to the Hall, where the entry was witnessed by certain members of the Entertainment Committee. The savoury mass was borne in festal triumph, decorated with the City Arms and

OX ROASTS – FROM FROST FAIRS TO MOPS

Figure 50. The Lord Mayor's baron is carved in ritual fashion. Steel engraving from The Illustrated London News. *13 Nov. 1887.*

Figure 51. A full baron of beef being roasted with a mechanical dangle-spit for the 1903 Christmas dinner at the Constitutional Club in London. This lithograph, which was published in the French magazine Illustration, *depicts a roasting hearth fitted with a very unusual integrated roasting screen. The caption reads 'in former times an entire ox was roasted at a wood fire in the enormous fireplace of the kitchens. The fireplace has now become a large metal closet of architectural pretensions, where a robust and complicated mechanism continuously turns the Pantagruelian roast.' The Constitutional Club was founded in 1833. It was formerly in Northumberland Avenue.* Illustration, *Paris, 26 December 1903, p. 434.*

Union Jacks; and was then deposited on a sort of pedestal at the foot of the Beckford Monument. At night 'the Baron' was cut up by the 'City Carver', whose exclusive office it is to dispose of the substantial luxury among the guests at the banquet; and we can assure the readers that incessant were the demands for 'the Roast Beef of England'.[47]

Whether at frost fairs, coming of age parties or jubilees, ox roasts were the time-honoured way of celebrating major events and milestones in local and national life. It is impossible to pinpoint how they started, but they may have had their origins in displays of hospitality to the poor by religious houses and benevolent landowners. They were street affairs and as such were the forerunners of the armistice and victory street parties of the twentieth century. However, the strong element of patriotism and nationalism they expressed also found a place in the way that our national dish was cooked and served in more palatial surroundings, such as those discussed in the next essay.

Figure 52. Many early ox roasts were charity events paid for by wealthy benefactors and public subscription. There were other 'roasting spectaculars' which fulfilled a similar role. On 'roast goose day' (29 September), the pensioners of the Old Men's Hospital in Norwich were treated to a feast of roast goose. Fifty-six geese were roasted at the same time on a single spit. When they were ready, the geese were quartered and distributed to the aged inmates. Steel engraving from The Illustrated London News, *8 Oct. 1859.*

NOTES

1. John Gay, *Trivia, Or, the Art of Walking the Streets of London* (London, 1716), II 368
2. Broadside, printed by David Hannot, *On the Ice, at the Maidenhead at Old Swan Stairs*, January 16th 1716. Author's collection.
3. Ian Currie, *Frosts, Freezes and Fairs* (Frosted Earth, London, 2002), pp. 1–15.
4. I am indebted to Nicholas Reed for drawing my attention to this painting. Its current whereabouts and owner are unknown. However, it is reproduced on a mid-twentieth century Christmas card, from which fig. 33 is taken. Nicholas Reed, *Frost Fairs on the Frozen Thames* (Lilburne Press, Folkstone, 2002).
5. *Great Britain's Wonder: London's Admiration*, printed broadside (London 1684).
6. *God's Works is the World's Wonder*, printed broadside (London, 1683).
7. *The Family Guide*, printed broadside – a price guide to butcher's meat (London, 1794).
8. Because both wood and coals had to be transported by road rather than up the river on barges during the hard freezes the price of fuel rose to exorbitant heights. In the severe winter of 1684, John Evelyn commented that 'all sorts of fuel so dear, that there were great contributions to keep the poor alive'. Fuel required for cookery on the frozen river also had to be carted across the ice by horse-drawn sledge.
9. *Great Britain's Wonder*….
10. Ibid.
11. Ibid.
12. Ibid.
13. *God's Works*….
14. Reed, p. 27.
15. George Cruickshank, *Thames Frost Fair*, lithograph 1814. Author's collection.
16. Henry Mayhew, *London Labour and the London Poor*, II (London; 1851), pp. 93/2.
17. *God's Works*….
18. William Hone, *The Every Day Book* (London, 1826), Vol. I, Part II, pp. 1482–86.
19. Robert Chambers, *The Book of Days* (London, 1864), II, pp. 224–26.
20. A lamb is drawn, in *Notes and Queries*, 6th Series, 7 (1883), 131–2.
21. Steve Roud, *The English Year* (Penguin, London, 2008), pp. 287–88.
22. *Notes and Queries*, 1st Series, vii, p. 358. Cited in George Laurence Gomme, *Ethnology in Folklore* (London, 1892).
23. Robert Burnard, *Transactions*, Devonshire Association, XVIII, 1896, pp. 99–102.
24. Theo Brown, 'The Folklore of Devon', in *Folklore*, Vol. 75, No. 3 (Autumn, 1964), p. 158.
25. William Gilpin, *The Life of Bernard Gilpin* (Glasgow, 1830), p. 187.
26. Gilpin, p. 189.
27. Hone, Vol. I, Part II, p. 1337.
28. Daniel Defoe, *Tour Through the Whole Island of Great Britain* (London, 1724 –27).
29. Francis Grose, A *Classical Dictionary of the Vulgar Tongue* (London, 1785).
30. Hone, Vol. I, Part II, p. 1337.
31. Roud, op. cit., pp. 338–9.
32. M.L. Stanton, J.B. Partridge and F.S. Potter, 'Worcestershire Folklore', in *Folklore*, Vol. 26, No. 1 (Mar. 31, 1915), p. 95.
33. *The Stratford-on-Avon Herald*, 17 Oct. 1907.
34. *The Jubilee of George the Third – the father of his people – an account of the celebration in the towns and villages throughout the United Kingdom of the forty-ninth anniversary of his reign, 25th October 1809* (Birmingham, 1810).
35. *The Jubilee of George the Third…*, 2nd Edition (London, 1887), p. 73.
36. *The Jubilee of George the Third…* (1810), pp. 26–27.
37. Op. cit., p. 27.

38. *The Jubilee of George the Third...* (1887), pp. 22–3. Photographs of late nineteenth century ox roasts show enormous stacks of loaves, sometimes cut carefully into uniformly thick slices for serving with the beef.
39. Ibid., p. 80.
40. Ibid., pp. 31–2.
41. Ibid., p. i.
42. A.P. Wadsworth and Julia L. de Mann, *The Cotton Trade of Industrial Lancashire 1600–1780* (Manchester, 1937), p. 331.
43. I am indebted to Mark Smith for generously sharing his research of this event. He has written a very full article on the affair in *NMMA Newsletter*, No. 21, Spring 2001. See also, *The Oldham Advertiser,* 27 November 1858.
44. Reed. op. cit., p. 18.
45. Gas was used for roasting oxen on a number of occasions during the nineteenth century. One was roasted in 1860 in the Cathedral Close in Exeter using a newly invented gas-fired roaster.
46. *The Jubilee of George the Third...* (1887), pp. 116–7.
47. *The Illustrated London News.* 13 Nov. 1847, p. 310.

CHAPTER THREE

THE ROAST BEEF OF WINDSOR CASTLE

Peter Brears

Roast Beef be the pride and glory of this happy island. Dishes simple in themselves, and easily prepared, mark the manners and morality of a nation. When England discards Roast Beef, we may fairly conclude that the nation is about to change its manly and national character.[1]

This was the opinion of Dr Hunter of York in 1806, reflecting that of most of his contemporaries. The role of roast beef as a national symbol had already become well established by the early eighteenth century. Henry Fielding's song 'Oh! the Roast Beef of Old England, And old English Roast Beef!' long survived his *Grub Street Opera* of 1731, still being popular in the music halls of Edwardian England.[2] The development of roast beef as a national dish may be followed by studying how it was cooked in the great medieval kitchen in the royal castle of Windsor. From the time it was rebuilt in stone by Edward III in 1331, this kitchen produced roasts almost continuously through to the early twentieth century. This remarkable 600-year tradition was not dependent on mere custom and practice however, but on the excellence of its product. All tender meats benefit from being cooked solely by radiant heat in a strong draught which carries away all their heavy and cloying elements. Enclosing them in hot metal boxes where they soak in the fumes of their over-heated fats is a decidedly second-rate procedure, its only benefits being those of economy and time-saving. This is why many great English households continued to use their massive open-fire roasting ranges through to the 1930s. Only then did the effects of death-duties and the Depression finally kill off the true 'Roast Beef of Old England'. Although it would be foolish to make any deeper connection, the decline in roast beef actually did mirror the decline of Britain as the world's greatest super-power, just as Dr Hunter had predicted.

Returning to medieval Windsor, here, as in all great households, beef was the most important meat. The bulk of it would be boiled to feed the lower orders who took their meals at the long tables in the great hall. Only the finest cuts of meat, poultry and game were roasted, often in separate kitchens, for the tables of kings, lords, knights, and others of high status. At Windsor, Edward II's cooks used a timber-framed great kitchen in the north-east corner of the upper bailey. It was flanked by a larder at one side and a bakehouse on the other, the heat of the latter keeping the King's crossbows dry in an adjoining store. At this period most of the beef was boiled in the great kitchen, where a boiling furnace was installed in 1312.[3] In 1331 Edward III rebuilt the kitchen in stone with no less than five fireplaces in its side walls, and others at each end. A new larder, pastry, dresser, and a salting house with three hearths or furnaces probably for boiling brines and beef, were added in the 1360s.[4] As might have been expected, that most epicurean of monarchs Richard II made further improvements to the Windsor kitchens. His 'Kitchen for the King's persons' would be where 'the chef Maister Cokes of Kyng Richard' cooked their 'curious potages & meates and sotiltees', as recorded in their great manuscript recipe book, *The Forme of Cury*. Here, along with plainer roasts, they would have prepared *cockagryce* (cock-a-pig) of a cockerel stitched to the rear end of a sucking-pig, *yrchons* (hedgehogs) or *potte wys* (flower-pots) both of pork forcemeat, or *hastelets of fruyt* (dried fruit and almonds spitted and basted with batter).[5] For cooking these, Richard Nicol, mason, built two *reredoses*, and Andrew Richard and his mates another, using six quarters of broken tile. These were firebacks, either free-standing or within chimney arches, which directed the radiant heat of the fire forwards, ideal for roasting.[6] In 1455 John Gourney, Master Cook for the King's Mouth, with three assistants, prepared all the food here for Henry VI, with six 'Children of the Kechyn, tournebroaches' to turn the spits before the fires.[7] Similar establishments were maintained by later medieval and Tudor monarchs.

It is only from the reign of Henry VIII that practical details of the roasting equipment used in royal palaces first becomes available. As seen in the painting of *The Field of the Cloth of Gold* (c.1545), and the surviving great racks still in place at Hampton Court Palace, the iron spits were over nine feet in length by around an inch in cross-section. At each end they were supported on an iron rack or cob-iron, these tall uprights having a

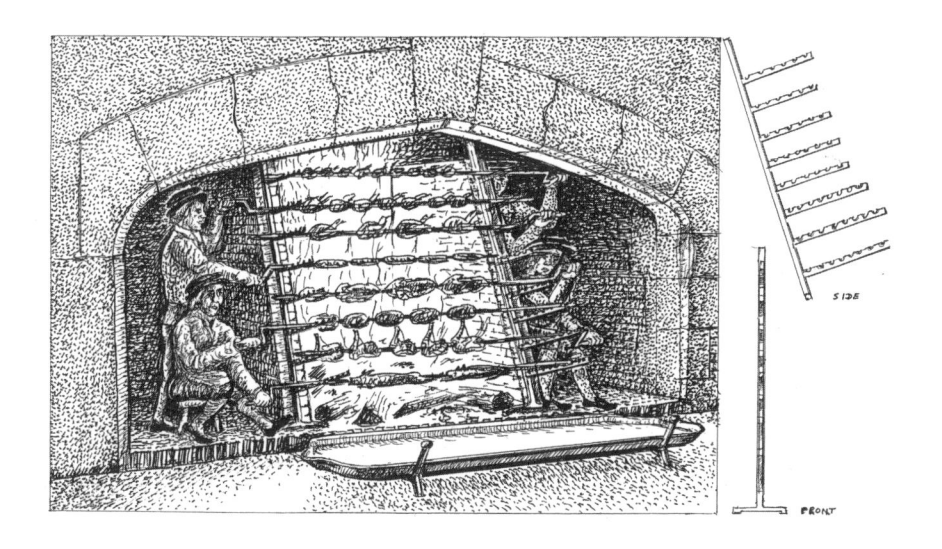

Figure 53. The roasting ranges (a) at Hampton Court, c.1530, and (b) at Kew Palace, c.1735. (Peter Brears)

Figure 54. The Great Kitchen, Windsor Castle, from a watercolour by J. Stephanoff, c.1820. This shows it still in its original form, as built by Edward III in the fourteenth century. Note the roasting hearths on the north wall (left) and east wall (centre).

Figure 55. The kitchen in 1856, from the west. It shows the smoke-hood and roasting screen designed by Sir Jeffry Wyatville as part of his great restoration programme in the mid-1820s.

cross-bar at the base to keep them vertical, and a wall sloping back at 20 degrees to hold them in place, retain the central fire, and provide shelter for the turn-spit boys.[8] Each rack had eight bars projecting from its front face, these having semi-circular notches cut in them so as to hold any spit in any of fifty-four different positions. Beneath lay a great iron dripping-pan, its ends forged into spouts from which to pour the hot fats for basting or other purposes. With one spit-turner standing, and another sitting before him at each end of the hearth, eight spits could be turned at once, giving some fifty feet of working spit-length within a single fireplace. Up to 1530 the kitchen staff habitually worked 'naked or in garments of such vileness, lying in the nights and dayes in the kitchens or ground by the fire-side'. To remedy this problem, Henry VIII provided the master cooks with a clothing allowance with which to keep the junior staff well and cleanly dressed. In addition the boys were to sweep the palace yards regularly, both to give them some fresh air, and to ensure that everyone could see just how clean they were.[9] Most of the meat they roasted in the lords-side kitchen would have been eaten by the leading courtiers and upper servants, that for the others dining in the great hall being boiled in the hall-side kitchen and the boiling house.

Under Elizabeth I, there continued to be two or three master cooks in the royal kitchens, one for the privy kitchen, cooking the Queen's food, and others for the lords-side and hall-side kitchens.[10] At Windsor, the privy kitchen was improved with a lantern or roof-light to give better illumination, new fireplaces, and an oven or furnace, while the great kitchen had its roof and chimneys repaired and re-leaded in 1577.[11] Although James I reduced the number of dishes served at his own and his household's tables, he continued to maintain and operate the royal kitchens as in previous reigns.[12] So did Charles I, until the progress of the Civil War saw the effective breakup of the traditional royal household. There was a proposal for the state to sell Windsor Castle during the Commonwealth, but fortunately it was rejected, Cromwell occasionally using it as an official residence. It is possible that the roasting ranges now prepared some of Mrs Cromwell's recipes, such as roast stuffed lamb or kid, mutton larded with herbed oysters, or with a dripping-pan of stewed Hackney turnips placed beneath it to absorb the dripping.[13]

After the Restoration, Charles II carried out a whole series of necessary extensions and repairs to the Windsor Castle kitchens. It was first intended to fully restore the traditional Bouche of Court, by which the royal kitchens fed everyone who attended the court, as well as the household officers and servants. In practice, this proved impossible, so the kitchens were reorganized to operate on a smaller scale. One of the changes, due to the increasing complexity of cookery and the lavish quantity of dishes required to serve the monarchs, was the great enlargement of the privy kitchen. In the late seventeenth century there were sixteen cooks in the King's privy kitchen, fourteen in the Queen's privy kitchen, and eleven in the household kitchen, the lords-side kitchen and the bulk of the household cooks having disappeared in the reorganization. Even so, there were still fourteen turnbroaches employed full-time to operate the spits.[14]

Of all the Stuart master-cooks, the most renowned was Patrick Lamb, who served successively Charles II, James II, William & Mary, and Queen Anne. As he himself recorded, 'his Name and Character are so well known and establish't in all the Courts of Christendom, that I need observe no more of him.' In addition to plain roasting beef, he also forced (stuffed) it:

> when your Beef is almost roasted, raise up the Skin or out-side of it, and take the Flesh of the Middle, which you must shred very small with the Fat of Bacon, and Beef, fine Herbs, Spices, and good Garnishings. With this you stuff your Beef between the Skin and the Bone, and sew it up very carefully to prevent the Flesh from dropping into the Dripping Pan, when you make an end of roasting it.

At table, the skin was removed, so that the beef could be eaten with a spoon.[15]

In the recipes of the first three Georges, roasting remained as popular as ever in the royal palace kitchens. When William Kent built a new kitchen for Kew Palace in 1735, he included a large open-fire roasting range. Its front was composed of nine square bars, all set horizontally, all but the top one on the diagonal in section, to allow the burning coals within to fully radiate their heat. The fireback was of iron plate, an adjustable cheek at either side allowing the length of the fire to be regulated as required. At each end of the range, the vertical iron posts were fitted with five horizontal bars notched to hold the spits in thirty six different positions. These were virtually identical to those used at Hampton Court two hundred years earlier, proving the long continuity of royal roasting tradition.

Figure 56. The kitchen in 1857, from the west, with the roasting hearth on the east wall. Here it is decorated for Christmas with evergreens and holly. Note the spectators in the southern turret.

By the 1780s, the great kitchen at Windsor Castle had been sub-divided by partition walls to form a suite of six separate rooms, each probably performing its own unique function.[16] Even the fireplaces on the end walls appear to have been blocked up, while two on the side walls had partitions built into them. A few years later all these accretions were stripped away to return the kitchen to its original medieval proportions. A finely-detailed watercolour by J. Stephanoff shows it in use about 1820 (fig. 54). In the centre, a man stands before a large set of beam-scales, checking the weights of the joints just delivered, while to the left the first fireplace on the north wall shows roasting in progress. The range is almost identical to that at Kew Palace, but now the spits are being turned by a smoke-jack, the updraught in the chimney rotating a vane mounted in the chimney flue. The motion is then transferred to a multi-grooved pulley, from which chains descend to pulley-ended spits supported on the horizontal spit-

Figure 57. A baron of beef in the western roasting hearth, after a painting by Frank Watkins, 1870s.

racks. No turnbroaches were required at this range, but they must have still turned the spits before the fire on the east wall, where no smoke-jack gear is to be seen.

Stephanoff's painting was made at a most opportune time, for the great medieval kitchen, still with its soot-stained whitewashed masonry walls, was now to undergo a major restoration. George IV was both epicure and connoisseur. In 1816, as Prince Regent, he had built the kitchens of Brighton Pavilion, having employed the greatest chef of his age, Antonin Carême, the previous year. In Carême's opinion,

> The essentials of English cooking are the roasts of beef, mutton and lamb; the various meats cooked in salt water, in the manner of fish and vegetables... fruit preserves, puddings of all kinds ... that is the sum of English cooking.

He returned to France in 1818, leaving behind a culinary legacy continued by those who had worked under him.[17] Having ascended the throne, George IV set about the improvement of all the royal residences. For Windsor Castle a scheme for the improvement of the royal suite in the upper bailey was costed at £150,000, for which Parliament agreed the appropriate budget. Along with many other great households, the defeat of Napoleon and the establishment of a new order in Europe and beyond provided the impetus for investing in massive new building programmes. As part of the works, Sir Jeffry Wyatville completely revamped the kitchen, making it extremely efficient and modern, yet retaining an overall medieval style. The general layout followed that introduced at Brighton Pavilion. In the centre stood a large steam-heated hot-table covered with a clean white cloth. This replaced the dresser of earlier days, keeping the cooked food ready for service, while the cloth showed up any smuts on the undersides of the dishes, so that they could be removed before they could stain the damask tablecloths 'upstairs'. An L-shaped table stood just beyond each corner of the hot-table, each holding the utensils for a master-chef. Between these stood pedestal tables with extending flaps, should additional workspace be required, while at one end there was a small octagonal table apparently used by one of the kitchen clerks when recording in fresh foodstuffs. Behind the L-shaped tables, the side walls were fitted with dressers and wall-racks all topped by long shelves to hold the vast *batterie* of copperware.

The former fireplaces were now filled with stoves, hotplates and ovens. For roasting Wyatville remodelled each end-wall with a central roasting range, its basic design identical to that at Kew, but fitted with more powerful smoke-jacks, and much more elaborate woodwork. Above each fireplace a large, gothic-style castellated smoke-canopy of oak was fixed against the chimney-breast. In front stood a huge oak roasting screen, also castellated, and decorated with carved roses and portcullises. Both its open interior which faced the fire, and the screen-doors which hinged out from each end, were clad in polished metal, to reflect the heat back onto the joints. The back, meanwhile, had sliding doors to give access to the iron shelves within, as it doubled as a huge hot-cupboard

The completed kitchen was illustrated and described in Frederick Bishop's *Wife's Own Book of Cookery* of 1856. He knew the royal household well, having served as *cuisinier* at St James's Palace. At Windsor, he appears to have seen all the preparations for Christmas Dinner, sixty turkeys being roasted over the season. The 'large fires at both ends of the kitchen look enormous, and, with the viands slowly revolving on the spits, present a wonderful picture.' An imposing central figure, without an apron, may represent M. Moret, *chef de cuisine*, who appears to be supervising his two master-cooks, two yeomen of the mouth, two yeomen of the kitchen, two roasting cooks, two larderers, five scourers, one steam-man to cook the vegetables, three kitchen maids, four apprentices, and two men in the adjacent green-office, who cleaned the vegetables. In contrast to the anger-producing haste of many modern restaurant kitchens there was great order and peace.

> The quiet is remarkable. The chief scene of activity is when the footmen are in attendance to convey the dishes from the hot table in the centre of the kitchen, on which they are disposed, to the apartments in which they are to be served.[18]

The same scene was illustrated by J. Brown in *The Illustrated Times* in 1857, but with the roasting screen removed to show the spits rotating before the roaring fire, and the lamp-standards and roof decorated with sprays of seasonal holly. 'Symmetrical rows of tables line the hall of Royal cookery: and here the white jacketed and white-capped cooks (assisted sometimes by smart young damsels) are busily employed putting the finishing touches to the dainty dishes that are to be set before the Queen' at Christmas.

In the 1870s, Frank Watkins of Feltham, Middlesex, was an aspiring but little-known artist, concentrating on moralistic paintings with titles such as *Know nor care, nor no married strife* or *Has wives many as he will, I would the Sultan's gay lot fill*.[19] In the 1990s his painting described as *A Country House Kitchen* was offered for sale by a London dealer and purchased by Gunnersbury House Museum. It was, in fact, a fine view of the roasting range at the west end of the Windsor kitchen. The details are closely observed, including the great oak wall-clock inscribed 'G. IV, REX 1829'. There is no evidence to suggest why, or for whom, the painting was commissioned, but since the kitchens were not open to the public, the well-dressed visitors were probably members of the royal family, come to inspect the Christmas baron of beef. This was a huge joint of around 130 lb, comprising two rumps, two sirloins and an extra rib on both sides.

Figure 58. This illustration from Pictorial World, *2 January 1875, shows a number of details not depicted elsewhere. These include the stay-bar which secured the spit-stand to the firebars, the guide frame for the jack-chain, and the highly reflective side-door of the roasting-screen, here folded back behind the cook on the right.*

Figure 59. The kitchens in 1894, from the east.

Figure 60. The western roasting range with Christmas roasts, 1894.

Figure 61. The western roasting range, with its smoke hood and roasting screen, after a photograph of 1898.

Having been spitted through the spinal channel, it was wrapped first in flour-and-water pastry and then in paper. Rotating three feet from the fire for twenty minutes, it was taken back to five feet, and continuously basted for the next eight or nine hours. Half an hour before finishing, the paper and pastry were removed in order to give the joint a fine golden colour.[20] It is this latter stage which is shown in the painting, with one of the roasting cooks, in his characteristic toque, carefully basting the joint.

The fact that the baron of beef was being roasted at Windsor was no indication that it was to be consumed there. In 1894, for example, 'The baron will be roasted at the great kitchen fire at Windsor Castle, and when cold will be sent to Osborne, where, with the boar's head and game pie, it will adorn the royal sideboard.' That year it had been cut from a fine West Highland bullock bred and fed in Windsor Park, purchased for the Queen by Messrs Webb & Sons, Her Majesty's purveyors. *The Illustrated London News* for this year carried two illustrations of 'The Queen's Christmas: The Kitchen, Windsor Castle'.[21] One shows the whole kitchen from its east end, while the other shows the western roasting hearth with a number of small roasts rotating on its spits.

In 1898 a young Swiss apprentice cook called Gabriel Tschumi joined the royal household. Unlike most cooks, he took the trouble to set down his memories of his almost fifty-four years' royal service, providing a unique record of the practices followed there in the last years of Victoria's reign. The staff structure was almost the same as in the 1850s, with the royal chef, M. Menager, eight master cooks, two pastry cooks, bakers, confectioner's chefs, larder cooks and roast cooks, with two assistant chefs, eight kitchen maids, six scullery maids, six scourers, and four apprentices. On his first day at Windsor, he found that,

> the kitchen reminded me of a chapel, with its high domed ceiling, its feeling of airiness and light, and the gleam of copper, well-worn and burnished, at each end of the room The copper glint came from the stew pans which were ranged on hooks in a vast half circle above each of the two coal fires. Each was numbered, and the moment it was no longer in use it was the scullerymaid's job to clean and polish it and return it to its place in case it was needed by one of the chefs … rows and rows of shelves (on the side walls) were neatly stacked with stew pans of smaller sizes, omelette pans and every conceivable item of kitchen equipment. The kitchens had some

of the discipline of the barracks room. There was hardly any conversation apart from the giving of orders connected with the dishes on which each master cook was working…

More roasting was done at Christmas than at any other time of year, for then a 130-pound baron of beef was roasted in front of the coal range, and it was such a sight that it attracted the interest of a great many townspeople when Christmas was spent at Windsor Castle. This was the case in 1898,

> … Some of the servants came to tell the chef that quite a crowd of people had collected in the hope of seeing the baron of beef roasting for Queen Victoria's table, and as a special favour he invited some of the younger ones into the kitchen. It was a cheerful place, for it had been decorated with evergreens a few days earlier, and the great fires roasting away at each end of the kitchen cast a rich light over everything. One young boy, son of one of the gamekeepers in Windsor Great Park, asked if he could be allowed to baste the beef as the chef was doing, and was delighted when his request was granted.[22]

Roasting on a smaller scale took place here on most days to serve the royal family, the household, or the state banquets for guests as diverse as the King of Roumania or the Gackwar of Baroda.[23] The established culinary traditions continued throughout the Edwardian era, but then went into rapid decline under George V, especially when the strictest rationing was enforced from the royal table down to the servants' hall during the First World War. It was during his reign that spits and open fires were finally replaced by gas ovens at Windsor Castle, ending a continuous tradition of at least six hundred years. As Tschumi commented,

> There is a great deal to be said for the modern kitchen methods, but I regretted particularly the end of cooking on a spit. This a method which brings out the finest flavour of meat, and a skilful cook knows the secret of basting can produce a far tastier joint than any cooked in an oven.[24]

From this time there have been no open fires in the Windsor Castle kitchens. Even so, this did not prevent the medieval kitchen from being burnt out during the great fire which swept through the state apartments on 20 November, 1992. After removing all the debris, and erecting temporary roofs, the Royal Household gathered together a restoration team involving English Heritage, project managers, architects, structural engineers, quantity surveyors, heating and ventilation engineers, and a huge team of specialist craftsmen and contractors. Following a scheme prepared by Donald Insall Associates as architects, the kitchen was restored. The great lantern of skylights was rebuilt, and the clock, tables, dressers and wall-shelves newly constructed to designs following those of the Wyatville restoration. The castellated hoods of the roasting hearths were also re-made to the 1820s design, standing over the iron roasting ranges which had survived the conflagration. With newly-painted walls and new pendant electric lighting, the great kitchen still retains much of its original character as one of England's most impressive historic kitchens. It is as amazingly light and airy as when first built, and even more efficient. Even so, it is unable to produce the open-fire spit roasts for which it was once so famous.

NOTES

1. A. Hunter, *Culina Famulatrix Medicinae* (York, 1806), 6.
2. H. Fielding, *Grub Street Opera* (1731), III ii.
3. Sir W.H. St.J. Hope, *Windsor Castle, An Architectural History* (1913), 95.
4. Ibid., 186, 187, 189, 193, 194, 55 9.
5. C. B. Hieatt & S. Butler, *Curye on English* (Oxford 1985), 20, IV 183, 1.
6. Hope, op. cit., 222–223.
7. *Household Ordinances* (Society of Antiquaries 1790), 21.
8. P. Brears, *All the King's Cooks* (1999), 127.
9. Ibid., 112–1.
10. *Household Ordinances*, 252–3, 287.
11. Hope, op. cit., 270, 275.
12. *Household Ordinances*, 99.
13. For the household arrangements of Protector Cromwell see R. Sherwood, *The Court of Oliver Cromwell* (Cambridge, 1977), 15, 35–36. For Mrs Cromwell's roasts, see D. Clinton, (ed.) *The Court and Kitchen of Elizabeth Commonly Called Joan Cromwell* (London, 1664; Cambridge 1983), 44, 66, 70, 71.
14. *Household Ordinances*, 397–8.
15. P. Lamb, *Royal Cookery* (1726 edition), 18.
16. Hope. op. cit., Plan 1.
17. A. Willan, *Great Cooks and Their Recipes* (1992), 144.
18. F. Bishop, *The Wife's Own Book of Cookery* (1856), 384.
19. J. Johnson, & A. Greutzner, *Dictionary of British Artists 1880–1940* (Woodbridge, 1999), 531.
20. T. Garrett, *The Dictionary of Practical Cookery* (1893), I 122.
21. *The Illustrated London News,* 22 December 1894, 777.
22. G. Tschumi, *Royal Chef* (1954), 32, 33, 72, 73.
23. Garrett, op. cit., II 807.
24. Tschumi, op. cit., 72.

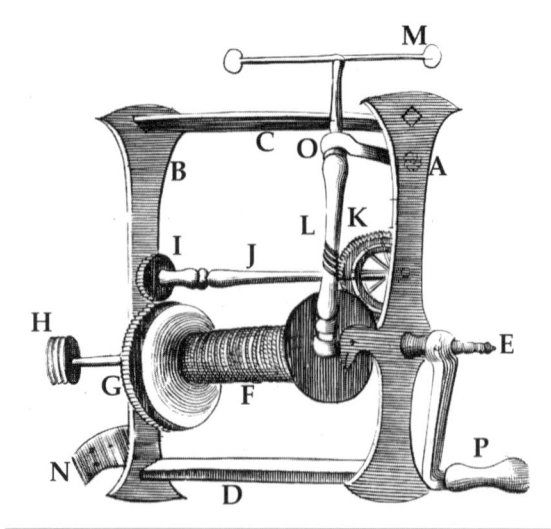

Figure 62. Anatomy of a common weight-jack.
Above. Woodcut illustration from Joseph Moxon, Mechanick Exercises or the Doctrine of Handy-Works *(London, 1678). In this book, Moxon, a member of the Royal Society, gives detailed practical instructions for fabricating a common two-spindle weight-jack.*
Below. A two-spindle English iron weight-jack dating from the late eighteenth century. This key is based on the text which accompanies the woodcut in Moxon. A: the fore-side; B: the back-side; C: the top-piece; D: the bottom-piece; E: the main-spindle; F: the barrel; G: the main-wheel; H: the struck wheel; I: the worm-nut or worm-pinion; J: the worm-wheel spindle; K: the worm-wheel; L: the worm; M: the fly; N: the stayes or back fastenings; O: the worm-loop (not visible in the photograph); P: the winch. Moxon called this mechanism a 'worm-jack' because of the 'worm' or endless screw L, which transmitted the motion to the fly M, which slowed down the descent of the jack weight. The 'struck wheel' H, transferred the rotary movement to a pulley on the end of a spit via a 'jack-chain' – see fig. 65 (top right). Photograph courtesy of David Hansord.

CHAPTER FOUR

THE CLOCKWORK COOK –
A BRIEF HISTORY OF THE ENGLISH SPRING-JACK

Ivan Day

> Gently stir and blow the fire,
> Lay the mutton down to roast,
> Dress it quickly, I desire;
> In the dripping put a toast,
> That I hunger may remove; –
> Mutton is the meat I love.
> On the dresser see it lie;
> Oh! the charming white and red!
> Finer meat ne'er met the eye,
> On the sweetest grass it fed;
> Let the jack go swiftly round,
> Let me have it nicely browned.
>
> from Dean Swift's *Receipt to Roast Mutton*.[1]

A clockwork jack turning rapidly on the chimneybreast, like that which roasted Jonathan Swift's mutton, was once a familiar sight in many British kitchens. Rotating spits by hand was a tedious, unpleasant job and the introduction from Europe of machines that could do the job instead, liberated many a drudge from the sweltering conditions of the roasting hearth. In his account of a visit to southern England in 1748, the Swedish naturalist Pehr Kalm, observed that 'Meat jacks, or spits, they have in every house in England. They are turned by a weight, which is drawn up as often as it has run down.'[2] Kalm was probably overstating his case a little, as culinary robots of this kind were in reality confined to fairly well-off households, but they were widespread.[3] Weight-jacks were by far the most common contraptions used for roasting in this country, but there were other automated ways of turning spits.[4] In some regions, notably the West Country and Wales, treadmills worked by small dogs were fairly common.[5] In some rare cases small waterwheels or even steam turbines were used.[6] Many kitchens in larger establishments were equipped with smoke-jacks, sometimes called air-jacks. These rotated the spits via a simple train of gears and pulleys, which were turned by the ascending heat of the fire acting on a vane fitted in the flue. Smoke-jacks may have come to England as early as the fifteenth century, though they are not described in literature or household inventories until the 1600s. Samuel Pepys described one owned by his neighbour John Spong which was made from wood.[7] Not surprisingly, no wooden examples survive in this country, but most visitors to country houses will be familiar with the metal smoke-jack mechanisms which grace the chimney breasts of many of our eighteenth- and nineteenth-century kitchens. Both smoke-jacks and wind-up weight-jacks were sold by ironmongers all over Britain and were frequently illustrated in their advertisements and trade cards. Smoke-jacks were the gas-guzzlers of the period kitchen, as they needed large amounts of fuel to function properly. They were also prone to failure unless there was a regular regime of cleaning and maintenance. They were only suitable for grander establishments and came into their own when very large quantities of meat needed roasting for ambitious entertainments. Some later models were capable of turning four or more horizontal spits at the same time, as well as a number of vertical dangle-spits.[8]

Weight-driven jacks were better suited to smaller roasting ranges and were commonly used in farmhouses, town houses and taverns, being known in Britain since the sixteenth century. Surviving examples from the seventeenth and eighteenth centuries usually have only two spindles and a worm and fly in the train and would have required a set of compound pulleys to slow down the descent of the weight. Examples on display in modern museum settings are frequently set up incorrectly, having the jack weight dropping directly to the floor without a pulley system, resulting in a frustratingly short running time. Later eighteenth- and early nineteenth-century examples worked more effectively because they had three spindles in the train, and required a less complex pulley arrangement to keep them going. Winding up the jack seems to have been an unpopular task, 'Servants object much to the trouble of winding up this jack, little as that trouble is; and hence smoke-jacks are suffered to supersede them, not

Figure 63. Detail of an advertisement for John Joseph Merlin's innovative Rotisseur Royal *of 1773. Merlin's invention was not only the first roasting jack in England to be driven by a wind-up clockwork motor, but also popularized the niche screen, which speeded up the roasting process by reflecting the heat back on to the joint. Courtesy of Science Museum/ SSPL. MS1728.*

withstanding their simplicity, and being less apt to be out of order.'[9]

Though used in Europe since at least the sixteenth century, jacks powered by wound steel springs instead of weights emerged rather late on the English kitchen scene. The earliest known appeared in 1773 and was marketed in London under the impressive French name *Le Rotisseur Royal*. It was a contraption designed to overcome some of the disadvantages inherent in the other types of jack. Unlike a weight-jack, it could be kept going for nearly two hours without complicated pulley systems, and did not require the regular and expensive oil changes needed to keep a smoke-jack running efficiently. Another feature which made the new jack very practical, was a large hooded tinplate screen designed to reflect the heat back on to the meat, reducing the roasting time by a third. This made

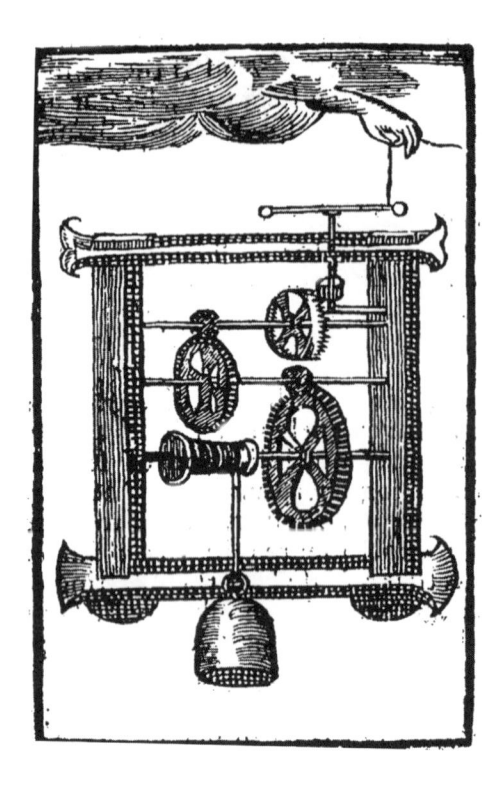

Figure 64. An early illustration of a weight-jack from John Wilkins, Mathematical Magic *(London, 1648). This woodcut illustrates an experiment in mechanics, which demonstrated that the spitjack's gearing would allow a weight as heavy as a man to be lifted from the ground by rotating the flywheel in reverse with a tied-on human hair.*

it much more economical of fuel than other jacks. The new jack was invented by the celebrated Belgian scientific instrument-maker Joseph Merlin (1735–1803) who was resident in London from 1760 to his death. Merlin had trained as a clockmaker in Paris, but applied his remarkable practical skills to many other disciplines. He designed and fabricated a harpsichord-pianoforte hybrid and made a number of important cellos. He is even credited as being the inventor of the roller skate. A well-known London eccentric, he drove round the city in a remarkable mechanical carriage decorated with images of the magician Merlin, a visual pun on his own name. Within a few years of arriving in England, he was working with the famous goldsmith, clockmaker and showman James Cox (*c.*1723–1800) on the movement of a perpetual motion clock and a number of very ambitious automata for Cox's mechanical museum in Spring Gardens. Though a foreigner and tradesman, Merlin moved in fairly elevated circles. His portrait was painted by Gainsborough and he socialized with the novelist Fanny Burney and her family. Merlin left James Cox's employment in 1773, when he realized that his boss was on the verge of bankruptcy. He

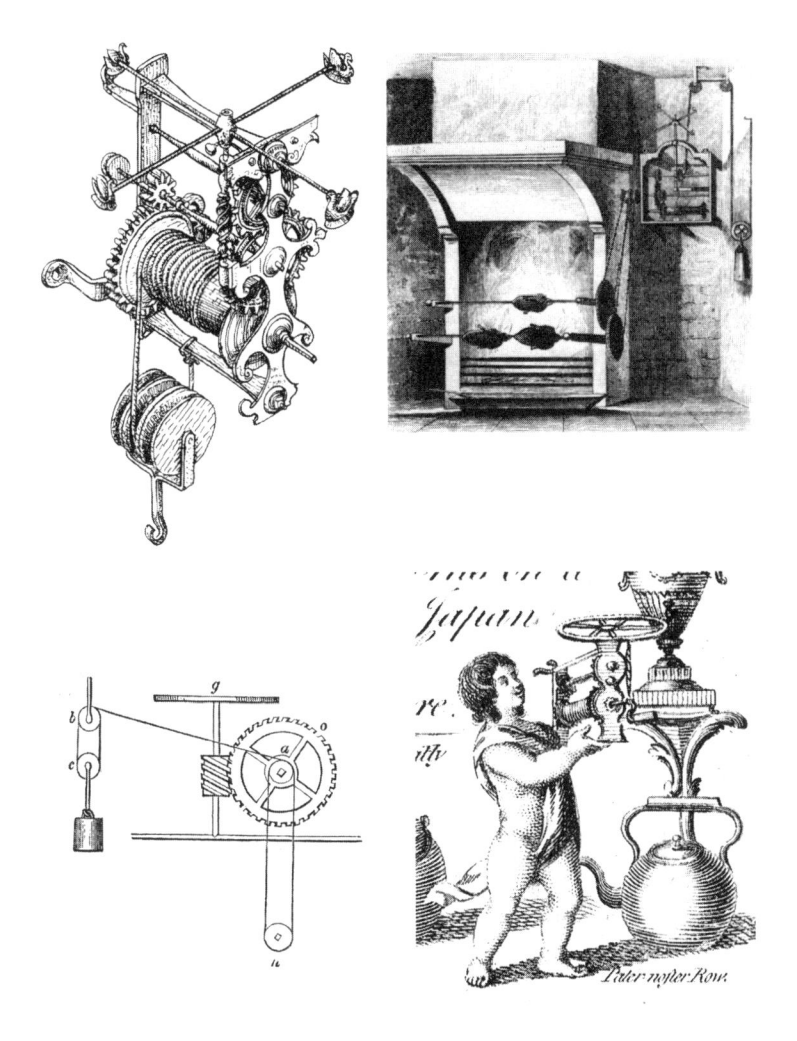

Figure 65. Top left. A three-spindle iron and brass English weight-jack with a brass fore-side engraved 'THO:/WILLS/ST AUSTLE. The fly has four lead weights in the form of swans. This jack survives with a compound pulley with three sheaves. Because of the extra spindle in the train, jacks like this were more efficient than simpler two-spindle models and required less complicated pulley systems. Torquay Museum V1475. Drawing by Peter Brears.
Top right. Though this illustration is of a French weight-jack (tourne-broche mural), it clearly illustrates how a three-spindle jack was set up with a system of compound pulleys with single sheaves. From Antoine Gogué, Les Secrets de la cuisine Française *(Paris, 1856).*
Bottom left. An illustration showing how the pulley system for a common weight-jack should be set up. The caption explains, 'a, is a barrel, round which is coiled a line of considerable length, and having one end fastened to a compound pulley, b c, containing three or four sheaves, to which is appended a weight, which, by descending slowly, moves the barrel round with the proper velocity'. From Thomas Webster, An Encyclopaedia of Domestic Economy, *new edition (London, 1847).*
Bottom right. A detail from the trade card of T. Ward, Ironmonger of 25 Newgate St., London c.1782. The putto is holding a common two-spindle weight-jack of the period. Sarah Sophia Banks Collection – BM 85.174. Courtesy of the British Museum.

was granted Royal Letters Patent for his *Rotisseur* in the same year, so the novel new jack seems to have been the inventor's first project after striking out on his own.

It is remarkable that a high-status maker of scientific instruments and fine clocks, who socialized with well-known members of London society, should turn his hand to manufacturing a product that would normally be associated with a lowly ironmonger. However, as a fabricator of precision-built timepieces and automata, he was probably astonished by the mechanical inefficiency and wasteful fuel requirements of most of the jacks used by English cooks.[10]

Because it was capable of being used in front of a much narrower fireplace than that required by the long horizontal spits run by weight-jacks and smoke-jacks, the *Rotisseur Royal* was highly suited to smaller kitchens and for shipboard and camp cookery. Merlin designed four different variations on his idea; two of which roasted the meat on long vertical spits; one on a short horizontal spit; while another was driven by an accessory he called a 'ventilator', rather than a clockwork engine. This was actually a rather eccentric smoke-jack mechanism with a turbine fitted in the chimney flue, which turned a long shaft, or arbor, connected to the top of the reflector. All four versions are illustrated on a 1773 advertisement and in somewhat more detail in the patent specification.

In Merlin's advertisement he explains that his newly invented machine was designed,

> for Roasting all kinds of Butchers Meat, Game, Poultry &c, & to bake Puddings, at the same time, being also a most convenient Plate warmer. The *Rotisseurs* are constructed on a principle entirely new, & also contriv'd as to roast any joint of Meat or other Article with one third of the Coals, consumed by the present mode of Cookery, & in less than two thirds of the usual Time. They are put in motion by a Machine fix'd at the head of the *Rotisseur*, which is constructed on the principles of Clock Work, & is made in so durable a manner, as to last many Years without repairs. The Machine being wound up sets the Spit going in the most regular manner for 2 hours in which time the largest Joint of Meat may be roasted; The *Rotisseurs* are made of Tin, which refracting the heat, roast quicker & gives the meat a finer flavour; There is a conveniency at the back for basting, & they are so light as to be mov'd at pleasure, & are extremely useful in Camp, or on

Figure 66. Roasting Range formerly in the kitchen of Chatsworth House. This very rare kind of jack was powered by a small waterwheel located in housing behind the dresser on the left. It was capable of running one horizontal spit and four vertical dangle spits. The latter could be moved in or out from the fireplace by adjusting the levers on the left jamb of the fireplace. The water which powered the jack was directed via a conduit from a pond on the hill above the house, which is still known as 'the jack pond'. The jack was removed when the fire surround was demolished in 1966 and its current whereabouts is unknown. However the wooden waterwheel survives in the Chatsworth kitchen. © Devonshire Collection, Chatsworth. Reproduced by permission of Chatsworth Settlement Trustees.

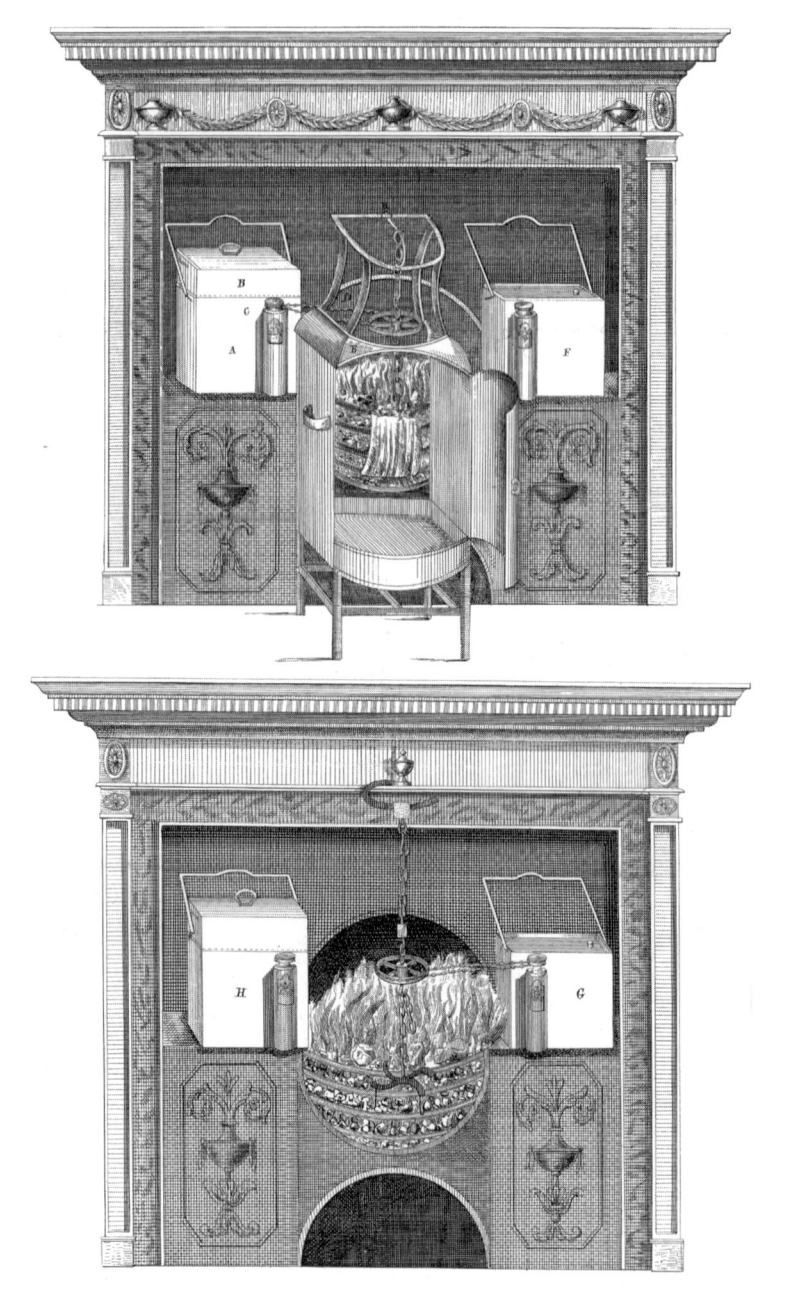

Figure 67. Steam Roasting Jack 1806. Chester Gould's design from Patent No. 2945. This unusual jack was driven by a steam turbine turning in a boiler (A, F, H and G). The rotary movement was transmitted to a suspended flywheel via a chain. It could be used with or without a niche screen. An additional steamer (B) could be placed on top to make use of the hot steam vented from the turbine 'for steaming vegetables and other purposes'. Gould's jacks were manufactured by his fellow patentees, the Birmingham scale-makers Thomas Bourne and William Chambers. Photo courtesy Intellectual Property Office.

Shipboard: The Price is from Two Guineas to 6, according to the Size of the *Rotisseur*, & the Elegance of its Construction; They are sold by the Patentee only, at No. 42 Little Queen Anne Street, Mary le Bone, who returns his most grateful Acknowledgements, to many of the Nobility and Gentry, who have honour'd his Invention with their warmest Approbation.[11]

Merlin seems to have manufactured his *Rotisseurs* for at least a decade, but unfortunately a surviving example has not yet come to light. The device however, possessed some key features which were to have a significant influence on English roasting techniques for well over a hundred years. The most important of these was the hooded tin reflector or niche screen. However, the combination of a screen with a jack was not entirely Merlin's own idea. Three years earlier in 1770, a Whitechapel glass dealer called Joseph Strutt had patented a portable stove with an integrated smoke-jack and meat screen.[12] In his specification, Strutt gives a very detailed description of the screen, which could be made of, 'tin, copper, or any polished metal, and the higher the polish the greater the reflection'. Merlin may have borrowed this idea from Strutt. Both inventors' screens had built in dripping-pans and trapdoors at the back for basting. These would remain important features of niche screens until they started to become obsolete in the early twentieth century, due to the eventual triumph of oven roasting.

Another feature described and illustrated in Merlin's 1773 patent was a suspended iron flywheel furnished with a number of small hooks, which he explained was, 'for the convenience of roasting a number of small birds at one at the same time.' Merlin may have got this idea from a smoke-jack designed in 1770 by Peter Clare, a professional jack-maker of Manchester, which featured a vertical dangle spit or 'rack-spit with twelve hooks by means of which twelve fowls or less may be turned at once'.[13] Clare's rack-spit was probably inspired by earlier non-mechanized dangle-spits. However, Merlin's hanging flywheel does seem to have been his own invention. It would become a very important feature of a number of later jacks, such as Chester Gould's 1806 steam-jack and just about every bottle-jack design used throughout the nineteenth century.

Merlin described the clockwork movement that ran the *Rotisseur* as a 'Spring Jack'. It was in fact a simple mechanism of a type commonly used since the Renaissance for powering the moving parts of automata, music boxes and other clockwork mechanisms. The famous Silver Swan automaton at the Bowes Museum in County Durham, on which Merlin worked with the goldsmith James Cox, is driven by a number of very similar devices. Merlin's spring-jack consisted of a train of gears run by a wind-up mainspring and an equalizing device called a fusee. In Merlin's specification he explained that the fusee could be connected to the drum containing the spring with either a chain or a length of catgut. The movement was regulated by a small fan flywheel.

Though they had been used on the Continent for at least two centuries, roasting-jacks driven by mainspring and fusee do not seem to have been known in Britain until Merlin introduced the *Rotisseur* in 1773. It is almost certain that this type of jack evolved in Italy during the sixteenth century or earlier. The oldest detailed illustration of a spring-driven machine, which is definitely a roasting-jack, appeared in 1570 in a recipe book written by the celebrated papal cook Bartolomeo Scappi, who called his mechanism a *molinello* (little mill).[14] It is likely that Scappi's illustration was intended to broadcast news of what was a recently invented, mechanically more sophisticated alternative to the weight-jack. In principle, the clockwork movement of Scappi's jack is identical to that used 200 years later by Merlin. However, Scappi had very little to say about the function of his machine and it is not until 1607 that a full description is given of the mechanism in Pietro Zonca's *Novo teatro di machine ed edificii* (Padova: 1607).[15] Zonca also provided a useful exploded diagram. The energy source for Zonca's *machina* was a wound steel spring attached to a stationary axle (arbor) enclosed in a steel barrel. The resulting motion was transferred by a rope to a cone-shaped pulley with a spiral groove carved all around – the fusee. The purpose of the fusee was to compensate for the weaker force of the spring as it wound down. This kept the mechanism rotating at a constant speed throughout the roasting process. Although it appears to have been used in clock movements from *c.*1430, the true origins of the fusee are unknown, though there is some evidence that it was part of a windlass for powering a crossbow as early as 1405.[16] The architect Filippo Brunelleschi (1377–1446) made a rough sketch of a fusee, as did Leonardo da Vinci (1452–1519). Neither offered any clues to the purpose of their mechanisms, though Leonardo's drawing does look suspiciously like a roasting-jack.[17] Like the fusee, the mainspring also seems to have first emerged in the fifteenth century, being used in locks before it was

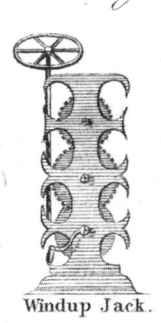

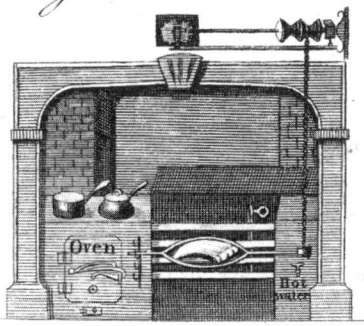

Figure 68. Above. Advertisment of Edmund Lloyd, ironmonger, 1801. Illustrated here are a three-pinion weight-jack, a smoke-jack and a bottle-jack and screen. The Sarah Sophia Banks collection, BM85.91. Courtesy of the British Museum.
Below. Smoke-jack formerly in the kitchen of Lowther Castle, Askham, Cumbria. It was made by Clement Jeakes in the 1890s for the Earl of Lonsdale. It was used on a number of occasions to roast meat for Kaiser Wilhelm II who stayed at the castle in 1911. It was probably the most ambitious smoke-jack ever manufactured in Britain. (Photograph private collection)

Figure 69. Handbill advertising some of Joseph Merlin's inventions, 1781–3. Those for which he received Royal Letters Patent are given pride of place – the Rotisseur Royal (top right) and his pianoforte-harpsichord (centre). Others are the gouty chair for infirm persons (top left), money scales (bottom centre) and two kinds of personal weighing scales (bottom left and right). Under the illustration of the Rotisseur is a caption which says, 'Please to observe ye thickest part of the Meat is always spitted upwards'. Photograph courtesy of Science Museum/SSPL. MS1728.

employed to run small clocks.[18] Mainspring and fusee mechanisms were used widely in the driving trains of early automata, such as the animated figures or jacks that performed on Renaissance tower clocks when the hour was sounded. They later became important components in watches. Both Scappi's and Zonca's mechanisms utilized flywheels identical to those on weight-jacks. These not only slowed down the train, but kept the system going, allowing a spit struggling with an unevenly balanced joint to complete its full rotation.

Despite a thorough search, no early-modern period *molinelli* of the kind illustrated by Scappi and Zonca have so far come to light in Italian museums and collections. However, a Dutch mainspring/fusee jack very similar in design does survive in the kitchen collection of the Museum Willet Holthuysen in Amsterdam.[19] The exact provenance of this mechanism is unknown, but the nature of the workmanship would indicate that it probably dates from the eighteenth century. Like the Italian mainspring-jacks, it features a coupling mechanism which allows the spits to be attached directly to the jack. However, unlike the roasting mills in Scappi's and Zonca's illustrations it utilizes a worm gear rather than a pinion to drive the flywheel. The author owns a seventeenth-century mainspring-jack of north Italian provenance, with an identical movement, but with a drive ending in a wooden pulley. The fusee in this mechanism is made from boxwood, which agrees exactly with Zonca's description, who explained that a fusee should be turned from box or pearwood. This jack is still in good working condition and will run for fifty minutes when fully wound. That so few of these mechanisms from this early period have survived in Europe would indicate that they never became a real rival to the much more widely used weight-driven mechanisms, despite the fact that they were very reliable and turned the spits in a uniform and regular fashion, even when the spring was winding down. Forging springs and making fusees, though a straightforward job for a professional clockmaker, would have been a fairly difficult task for the lowly smiths who were the main manufacturers of jacks.

Merlin was the first instrument-maker in England to own a fusee engine, a complicated machine tool for cutting the spiral groove around the conical body of a fusee. The evidence for this is in Thomas Hatton's *An Introduction to the Mechanical Part of Clock and Watch,* published in London in 1773, the same year that Merlin was granted the patent for his *Rotisseur*. We learn from Hatton that a fusee engine had been made by 'Mr Merling, artist to Mr Cox'. This labour-saving engine was first described by the Swiss chronometer-maker Ferdinand Berthoud, who gave a full specification and diagram of the mechanism in *Essai sur l'Horlogerie* (Paris, 1763). Merlin worked in Paris between 1754 and 1760 when the fusee engine was being developed and it is possible that he learnt to make such a machine at that time. On the other hand, he may have fabricated one himself by following the very precise instructions and working diagrams in Berthoud's book. Whatever the truth, it is certain that Merlin introduced the fusee engine to the English clockmaker's workshop. Unlike the hardwood fusees of Renaissance jacks, those in Merlin's *Rotisseurs* were probably turned from brass. Having a machine tool that could readily mass-produce fusees may have been one of the reasons why Merlin decided to manufacture roasting-jacks with a spring-driven movement. It is likely that Merlin had seen them in his native Belgium, or in France, and recognized an opening in the London market for precision-built jacks of this kind. Some of Merlin's other inventions were also adaptations of French ideas, such as his gouty chair (a prototype invalid carriage) and his mechanical chariot, which he modelled on the French *post chaise*. It is likely that Merlin enlisted other tradesmen to make up the various components of the *Rotisseur*. There were scores of tinsmiths and skilled mechanics with workshops in London at this time and components could easily be sourced quickly.

A number of English jack-makers took up Merlin's idea of using a mainspring-driven jack housed at the top of a screen. Like him, some concentrated on developing mechanisms which rotated the meat vertically to suit the narrower hearths of the period. The most important of these was the London watchmaker William Freemantle of Aldersgate Street, who in 1790 patented an *Improved Vertical Spring Roasting Jack*. Unlike, Merlin's jack, Freemantle's device did not include a fusee in the train. It was a much simpler contraption with a silk cord suspension regulated by a verge escapement. Freemantle also designed a version which was driven by a suspended weight, rather than a spring. His verge-regulated weight-jack did not catch on, but the Improved Vertical Spring Roasting Jack was rapidly imitated and further developed by other jack-makers.[20] The movements of these mechanisms were usually enclosed in a metal cylinder, while the cord suspension was hung inside a long narrow tube on top of the cylinder. This gave the device a shape similar to that of a bottle, which

THE CLOCKWORK COOK

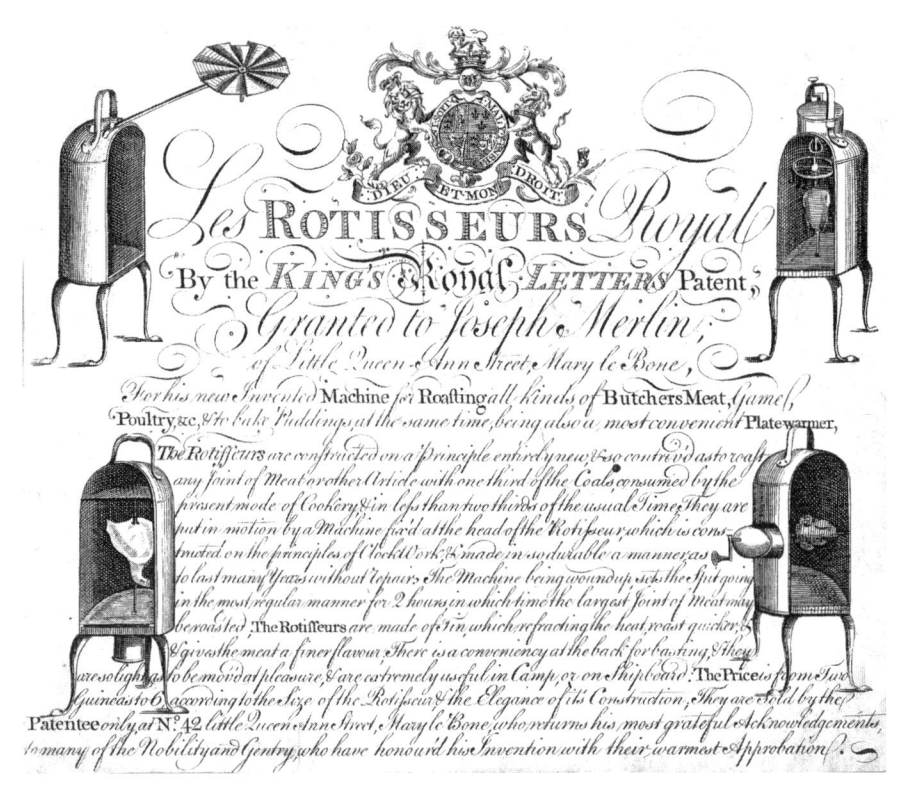

Figure 70. Advertisement for Joseph Merlin's Rotisseurs Royal *c.1773. Ambrose Heal Collection BM 85.194. Photograph courtesy of the British Museum.*

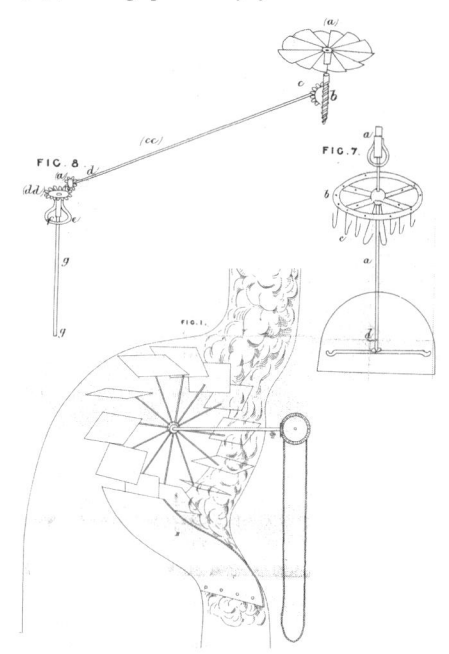

Figure 71. Above left. Merlin's 'ventilator' movement – an eccentric smoke-jack arrangement with an arbor that transfers the movement of the vane in the flue directly to a vertical spit in the niche screen.

Above right. Merlin's flywheel with meat hooks. When used in the rotisseur *this was attached to a long vertical spit. However, by the early nineteenth century it became the standard arrangement for regulating a bottle-jack with a light joint. Both drawings were made by Malby and Sons from Merlin's original drawings.*

Below left. A design for a smoke-jack by Joseph Braithwaite (1795). Unlike Merlin's more conventional 'ventilator' Braithwaite's vaned wheel rotated in the chimney flue on its horizontal axis, rather like a water wheel. It was intended to be a low-maintenance smoke-jack as it did not require the usual oil reservoir. Courtesy of Intellectual Property Office.

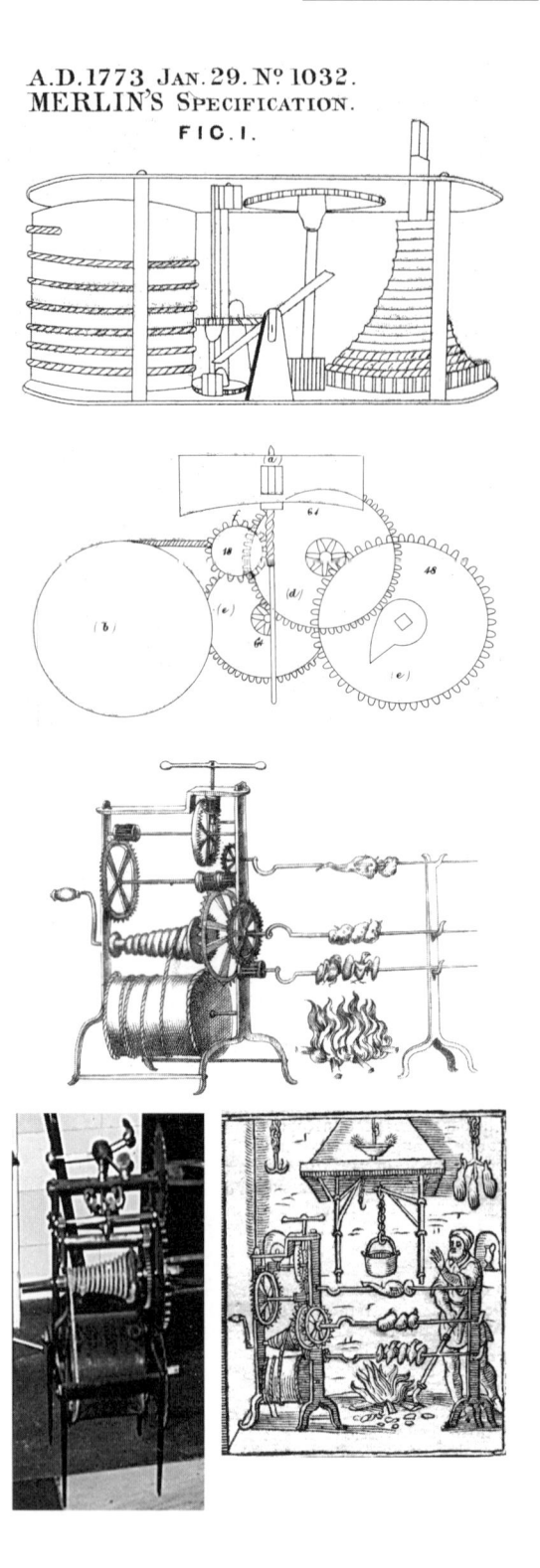

Figure 72. Merlin's Rotisseur movement. *A drawing made in 1856 by Malby and Sons from Merlin's patent specification of 1773. The original is a watercolour, almost certainly executed by Merlin himself. The four-wheel mainspring/ fusee movement has a fan fly and is almost identical to the much earlier jack mechanisms illustrated in figures 73 and 74. Courtesy of the Intellectual Property Office.*

Figure 73. Top. Molinello con tre spedi *(roasting mill with three spits) from Bartolomeo Scappi,* Opera, *1570.*
Bottom left. A Dutch spring-jack *(*mechanisch broadspit*) very similar to that in Scappi's illustration. Photograph courtesy of Amsterdam Historic Museum.*
Bottom right. A molinello *in use in a Renaissance kitchen – from the title page of the 1621 Venice edition of Scappi's* Opera.

eventually led to them being called bottle-jacks. During the course of the nineteenth century, they were manufactured in industrial quantities and became the most widely used of all jacks in Britain. They were the only kind of jack unique to this country, being completely unknown on the Continent. From an early stage in their development, bottle-jacks were frequently used in conjunction with a flywheel equipped with small sliding hooks, identical to that designed by Merlin. Thomas Webster, the nineteenth-century writer on domestic economy, observed that the bottle-jack 'is capable of roasting a tolerably large joint; but if the joint be small and light, a weight of cast iron is necessary to be attached, to make it turn steadily.'[21] Webster illustrated the wheel and his drawing shows a number of small hooks, an arrangement identical to that first described in Merlin's 1773 specification. As well as Merlin's intended purpose of roasting small birds, these hooks also proved useful for suspending small pieces of bacon fat over the roasting meat, an ingenious automatic basting technique. Bottle-jacks were commonly used without niche screens, a practice which many preferred,

> Some cooks say that a bottle-jack is best used without the screen, or only one of the common kind, when the fire is large; for, with its own niche screen, the reflection is so powerful, that the meat is apt to be dried up too fast. The whole apparatus is extremely useful where the economy of fuel is to be much regarded; for it will roast very well, with attention, when placed before a very small fire in the range; and therefore it is much used in small families.[22]

Although Merlin's original invention was aimed at the kitchens of the nobility and gentry, the combination of jack and screen became popular much lower down the social scale. In 1801 Edmund Lloyd, a London iron-monger, advertised his bottle-jack and screen as a 'Cottage Jack'. A hundred years later, in 1901, the Birmingham-based firm of Alfred Bennet was still aiming the bottle-jack and screen at the same market. Bennett's 'New Cottage' jack and oven was sold in three sizes, the smallest costing 11/6d.[23]

In 1807, the London mechanic Edward Shorter patented a fusee-jack more or less identical to Merlin's, but with an additional, rather unusual component. Instead of driving the fly with a worm and worm wheel, Shorter explained,

> I do fix a small wheel upon the fly arbour, and do drive the same by another wheel applied thereto, not by the intervention or mutual action of teeth, but by the mere opposition of one surface against another, in which case the friction or stickage at the faces of contact is sufficient ... I do, in some cases, face the said wheels with buff leather, or with short hair standing out in the manner of a stiff brush.[24]

However, none of Shorter's 'hairy wheel jacks' seem to have survived. Another London jack retailer influenced by Merlin was the furnishing ironmonger Henry Marriott of 64 Fleet Street. In the first decade of the nineteenth century Marriott marketed a jack which contained a clockwork mechanism similar to Merlin's specification.[25] He explained that this device was 'constructed so as to require neither Line, Weights or Pullies'. Although Marriott did patent a number of other inventions, the patent documents have not survived for his jack. However, he constantly referred to it as the Patent Roasting Jack in his advertising literature. It is not known exactly when it first appeared. Nevertheless, the jack is illustrated on a trade card of 1809, so must have been launched some time prior to that date (see frontispiece).[26] It was designed to be flexible and could be fixed to the side of the chimney breast like a conventional weight-jack, or alternatively, attached to the top of a niche screen like Merlin's *Rotisseur*. There are at least three surviving examples in museum and private collections. One, which was displayed in a 1985 exhibition at Kenwood House, is screwed on to the top of a niche screen and arranged to rotate the joint from a suspended hook in exactly the same way as a bottle-jack.[27] When attached to a chimney breast Marriott's jack was capable of running three vertical dangle spits as well as two horizontal spits, a characteristic common in smoke-jacks, but not possible with conventional weight-jacks.

Unlike the standard weight-jacks of the period with their exposed movements, both Merlin's and Marriott's jacks were enclosed in sealed outer casings. These concealed the workings and prevented the accumulation of dust. The fusee in a Marriott jack in the Museum of London is wound with cat gut, a material sensitive to the effects of atmospheric humidity. This may be what Marriott was referring to on his 1809 trade card when he explained, 'the Works all being enclosed are protected from Injury, Irregularity and the weather, likewise not liable to be out of order, consequently well adapted for the use of Ships & Camps'. The dust created by raking out fires and

THE CLOCKWORK COOK

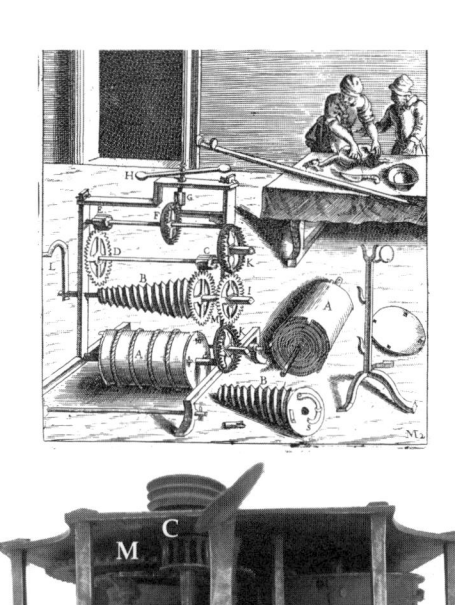

Figure 74. Anatomy of a renaissance spring-jack.
Top. Machina da voltar spiedi (Machine for turning the spits). The usual name for a jack at this period was a *voltaspiédi*. The modern Italian name is girorosto. From Pietro Zonca, Novo teatro di machine ed edificii, *Padova, 1607.*
Bottom. A late seventeenth-century Italian voltaspiédi *with a mainspring/fusee movement. The photograph has been taken from directly above the mechanism. The following key follows that of Zonca, but is much simplified. A: mainspring barrel; B: fusee; C: drive wheel pinion; E: worm wheel pinion; F: worm wheel; G: worm (not visible in photograph); H: fly – the fly in Zonca's illustration is a weighted fly, that in the jack in the photograph is a fan-fly with vanes that can be adjusted to slow the jack down by air resistance; M: main wheel.*

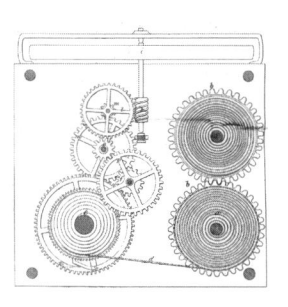

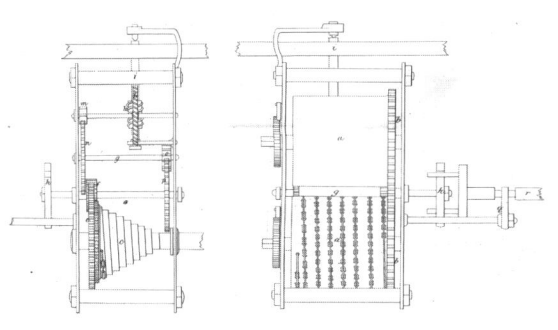

Figure 75. William Lane's design for the movement for his Improved Spring Jack of 1821. In principle, it is more or less identical to Merlin's jack, but for extra running time and power has an extra spring-barrel in the train. Courtesy of the Intellectual Property Office.

117

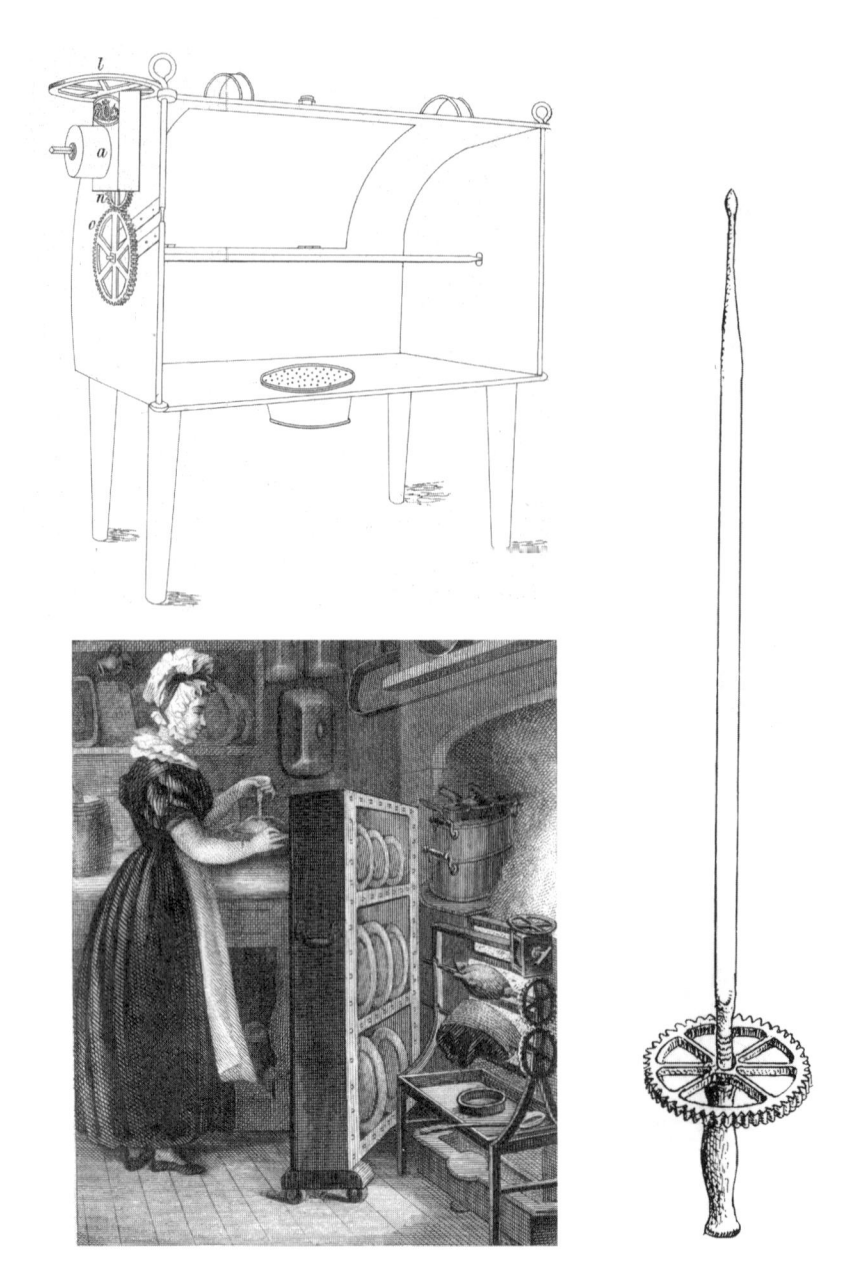

Figure 76. John Pearse's improved spring-jack of 1822. Top. Pearse's original design. Unlike Merlin's Rotisseur, Pearse's mechanism was designed to drive a horizontal spit. Patent No. 4693. Courtesy of Intellectual Property Office.
Lower right. In later versions of his jack, Pearse fitted a wooden handle to the spit to prevent the cook's hands from being burnt when he disengaged the hot spit from the jack movement. Drawing by Peter Brears.
Lower left. A version of Pearses' jack with two spits, but without an integrated screen. The cook is protecting herself from the heat and warming the plates with a common meat screen – from Elizabeth Hammond, Modern Domestic Cookery, *sixth edition (London, 1824).*

the small globules of airborne grease common in working kitchens had a detrimental effect on weight-jacks, whose clockwork trains were usually fully exposed. This dirt tended to accumulate on the wheels and pinions and caused them to run erratically. It was probably common practice to cover jacks when not in use. For instance, a 1762 farmhouse kitchen scene painted by Johann Zoffany, depicts an idle jack on the chimney breast protected with a cloth.[28]

During the course of the nineteenth century, many improvements were made to spring-jacks. In 1821, William Lane, a jack-maker of Birmingham, modified Merlin's movement by putting an additional spring barrel in the train. He explained, 'I do not claim any of the parts in themselves as new, but rest my Invention merely in combining of several spring barrels together by means of geer, so as to employ the united power or effect of several springs to produce a rotary movement.'[29]

A spring-jack with an integrated dripping-pan and screen was patented in 1822 by John Pearse, who described himself as 'Ironmonger, Clock and Watchmaker of Tavistock in Devon'. In his patent specification, Pearse explained that the device combined,

> a train of tooth'd wheels with a spring barrel, so as to produce a regular and continued rotator movement without the employment of a fuzee or chain. This improved spring jack is very small compared to its power, is simple in its construction and is perfectly capable when wound up of turning a joint of meat weighing 25lb and continuing to go from 30 to 40 minutes without requiring to be attended. Having described the various parts, wheels, pinions &c. of the mechanism, I wish it to be understood, that I do not claim them individually as my Invention, but merely their combination to the purposes of a spring roasting jack, the particular features of my Invention being the combination and operation of the train without a fuzee, and the connection of the spit to this train by means of a tooth'd wheel; which particular, being to the best of my belief new or never before employ'd in connection with a spring roasting jack.[30]

One of Pearse's mechanisms survives in Torquay Museum, though without its screen, which probably rusted away many years ago. However, one of its purpose-made spits does survive with its 'tooth'd wheel'. The spit is also equipped with a useful wooden handle to ensure that it could be removed from the screen without burning the cook's hands.[31] Pearse's new movement was compact, yet powerful. Without a fusee, the simplicity of its train leant itself readily to mass production. A version of it without an integrated screen was illustrated in the sixth edition (1824) of Elizabeth Hammond's *Domestic Cookery* where it is shown being used with a common meat screen. So within a few years, awareness of the Devon-based ironmonger's invention was reaching a national audience. It was not long before Pearse's jack was being imitated by other manufacturers. In the 1840s very similar devices were illustrated in a number of cookery books published by Longman, Brown, Green and Longman. These were described as having lately appeared, 'A box on top contains the spring, which carries round a wheel on the front; round this an endless chain passes over two pulleys to the spit, which goes through the side of the tin screen.'[32]

Pearse's jack was still being marketed in the late nineteenth century under the name of 'John Linwood's Improved Veruvolver'. Linwood's company, which had been the leading manufacturer of bottle-jacks in the first half of the nineteenth century, was taken over by Edward Bennett after Linwood's death in 1840. Edward was succeeded by his son Alfred.[33] These late Victorian horizontal spring-jacks were the direct descendants of Scappi's *molinello* and Merlin's *Rotisseurs*. However, they never became as popular as the bottle-jack and surviving examples are very rare.

In the earlier period of jack-making in Britain, a few clockmakers fabricated weight-jacks, but they were generally made by smiths and specialist jack-makers. From the time of Merlin onwards, an increasing number of English clockmakers, watchmakers and mechanics applied themselves to the design and improvement of spring-driven jacks. Mass production of these devices became more widespread as the Industrial Revolution progressed. At this time in France and Italy, scores of small factories also produced huge quantities of wind-up spring-jacks with horizontal spits for roasting modest sized joints and fowl, some with integrated reflectors. These were designed for wood-burning kitchen fireplaces of cottages and farmhouses and are still commonly found in junk shops, particularly in France. In nineteenth-century England, where coal was the most commonly used fuel for open-fire roasting, the eternal quest for economy resulted in a narrowing of the fireplace. Vertical roasting with a bottle-jack became the preferred method. As a result spring-jacks with long spits were probably never very common. The final demise of open-fire roasting in Britain was brought about by the emergence of the fuel-efficient closed range. The oven door finally closed on the Roast Beef of Old England in the decades around the time of the Great War and the vast majority of jacks, whether weight, smoke or spring ended up in the scrap metal yard.

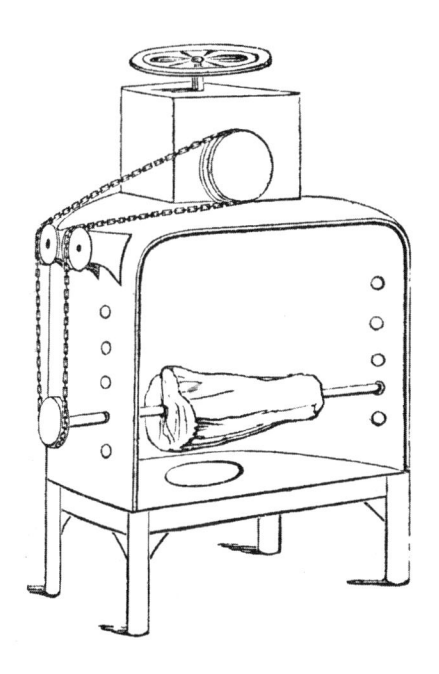

Figure 77. A horizontal spring-jack and screen with chain transmission of unknown manufacture illustrated in Eliza Acton, Modern Cookery *(London, 1845). A very similar device was illustrated on the trade card of William Peters and Son of Bristol, 1830. See Eveleigh in* Folklife *29, p. 17. Blaise Castle House Museum, T8291.*

NOTES

1. Quoted in William Kitchener, *Apicius Redivivus; Or, The Cook's Oracle* (London, 1817).
2. Pehr Kalm, *Visit to England 1748*, translated by Joseph Lucas (London, 1892).
3. David J. Eveleigh, '"Put down to a bright clear fire." The English Tradition of Open-Fire Roasting', in *Folklife* 29 (Leeds, 1991), p. 10. Through an analysis of probate inventories from 1568–1750, which included references to roasting equipment, Eveleigh points out that ownership of jacks was from 41% to 52%.
4. Jacks driven by means of a weight attached to a rope wound around a drum have been used extensively in most European countries since the Renaissance and possibly earlier. The earliest record of the ownership of a jack in England is in the 1587 inventory of William Hyde of Urmston, Lancashire (*Lancashire and Cheshire Wills* – Chetham Society, 1860, p. 190). They almost certainly evolved well before the mainspring-fusee jack. Early examples are difficult to date, though one of alleged sixteenth-century provenance is displayed in the kitchen of Raphael's House in Urbino in Italy – (Casa Natale de Raffaello, Via Raffaello 57, Urbino). However, many appear to be no older than the seventeenth century. A very large jack surviving in the kitchen of the Hôtel de Dieu in Beaune, France is known to have been installed there in 1698. The French name *tourne-broche* or *tourne-broche* is not included in Randal Cotgrave's *French Dictionary* (1611), who calls the mechanism a *tournerot*, which he translates as *a turne-roast or turne-spit*. Some French and Italian weight-jacks featured alarm systems that sounded a bell when the weight approached the floor.
5. Eveleigh, pp.7–10. Employing animals to turn spits seems to have been universal. In 1551, the Ottoman scientist Taqi al-Din invented a steam turbine to run a spit, 'so that it will rotate by itself without the power of an animal.' – *The Sublime Methods of Spiritual Machines,* quoted in Ahmad Y. al-Hassan, *Taqi al-Din and Arabic Mechanical Engineering* (Institute for the History of Arabic Science, Aleppo University, 1976), pp. 34–35. They were also used in Italy. John Florio in his *Italian Dictionary* (London, 1611), gives a definition of the word *molinello* as 'a wheel for the Dog to turn the spit in'. During the nineteenth century, dogs were even used in the United States to turn spits in restaurant kitchens. Henry Bergh (1811–1888) the wealthy founder of the American Society for the Prevention of Cruelty to Animals campaigned against their use. On more than one occasion when checking restaurant kitchens, he discovered that the dogs had been replaced by black children. Pace, Mildred Mastin, *Friend of Animals: The Story of Henry Bergh* (New York, Charles Scribner's Sons, 1942).
6. A steam-powered jack was installed in the kitchens of the Reform Club in 1840 under the directions of Charles Barry for Alexis Soyer. Mechanisms of this kind have a very long theoretical history, but do not seem to have ever gained much popularity. In 1551, the Ottoman scientist Taqi al-Din described a basic steam turbine that could turn a roasting spit (see citation in note 5). In England a steam turbine utilized to turn spits was mentioned by John Wilkins in *Mathematical Magic* (London, 1648) p. 149, 'They may also be contrived to be serviceable for sundry other such pleasant uses, as for the moving of sails in a chimney corner, the motion of which sails may be applied to the turning of a spit, or the like'. In 1793, a patent for a steam-powered spit was granted to the American inventor Samuel Morey (1762–1843). Morey's patent (US Patent No. 0000X51) was signed by both George Washington and Thomas Jefferson. Morey had competitors, as the following advertisement appeared in the New York *Evening Register* of 16 April, 1794, 'Baileys New Invented American Patent Steam Jacks, for sale by Browne and Pearsall no 248 Queen Street.' One of Bailey's steam-jacks survives in the Smithsonian Institute. In England the earliest manufactured steam-jack seems to be that of Chester Gould (fig. 67).
7. 'After supper we looked over many books, and instruments of his, especially his wooden jack in his chimney, which goes with the smoke, which indeed is very pretty' (Samuel Pepys,

Diary, 23 October 1660). Although there do not seem to be any surviving wooden smoke-jacks, the author has seen two weight-jacks made entirely from wood. Both were French and dated from the eighteenth century. The earliest English illustration of a smoke-jack is in John Wilkins, *Mathematical Magic* (London, 1648), pp. 149–152. Wilkins suggests that as well as roasting meat the device could be used 'for the reeling of yarn, the rocking of a cradle, with divers the like domestick occasions'.

8. An early example of a smoke-jack designed to run both horizontal and vertical spits was that invented in 1770 by Peter Clare, a Manchester jack-maker (Patent No. 975, AD 1770). However, it was a complicated mechanism and was much improved upon in 1795 by John Prosser of Holborn, who designed a more practical smoke-jack with much simpler mechanics (Patent No. 2064, SF 1795). Prosser modified his design in 1806, replacing the standard wooden chain pulley with a brass one with 'run tags' (small teeth), which stopped the chain from slipping, a common fault with most jacks (Patent No. 2982, AD 1806). Orthodox smoke-jacks had a vane which rotated in the flue around the vertical axis (like a helicopter). However some were designed with a vaned wheel which revolved in the horizontal axis (like a water wheel). The earliest of these was invented by Joseph Braithwaite, an engine-maker of Saint Pancras and is illustrated in figure 71 (Patent No. 2065, AD 1795). A more practical design for a similar mechanism was patented by the Edinburgh architect John Thin in 1825. Thin's jack was elegantly simple and unlike most smoke-jacks functioned without an oil reservoir.

9. Thomas Webster, *An Encyclopaedia of Domestic Economy*, new edition (London, 1847), p. 634. Very little is written about how weight-jacks were set up with pulley systems. However, an eighteenth-century two-spindle jack survives in Strangers Hall, Norwich (Norfolk Museums Services) with its full set of compound pulleys. In the painting *Distraining for Rent* (1815) by Sir John Wilkie (National Gallery of Scotland), a stone jack-weight suspended from a set of compound pulleys is depicted hanging in the corner of a kitchen. The Holborn engineer James White designed a number of improved pulley systems for weight-jacks, some of which he patented in 1788 (Patent No. 1650).

10. Merlin was not the only inventor who felt that roasting meat with jacks was wasteful of fuel. His contemporary, the American-born scientist Benjamin Thompson, better known as Count Rumford (1753–1814) was horrified by the amount of coal burnt in open-fire roasting and advocated doing away with the method altogether. In 1795 he introduced an enclosed cylindrical oven from Munich, which he called a 'roaster'. This enabled a draught of hot air to be blown over the meat to replicate the kind of effect achieved by roasting meat in front of the fire. He installed one of his 'Economic Roasters' in the kitchen of the London Foundling Hospital to demonstrate how a large quantity of meat could be roasted with a very small amount of fuel. There is also a good account with detailed drawings of Rumford's invention in Peter Brears, 'Kitchen Fireplaces and Stoves', in Sambrook., P. and Brears, P. (editors), *The Country House Kitchen 1650–1900* (Sutton, Stroud, 1996), pp. 107–109.

11. Trade card of Joseph Merlin, British Museum Ambrose Heal Collection 85.194.

12. J. and J. Strutt's Specification. Patent No. 964, AD 1770.

13. Peter Clare's Specification. Patent No. 975, AD 1770.

14. Bartolomeo Scappi, *Opera* (Venezia, 1570). *Molinello* was a general name for any small mill, but it could also more specifically mean a dog wheel. John Florio – 'a wheel for a dog to turn the spit in'.

15. Pietro Zonca, *Novo teatro di machine ed edificii per varie e sicure operationi, cō le loro figure* (Padova 1607), pp. 89–90.

16. Lynn White, *Medieval Technology and Social Change* (Oxford University Press, New York, 1966), pp. 127–128

17. Frank Prager, *Brunelleschi: Studies of his Technology and Inventions* (M.I.T. Press, Cambridge MA, 1970). See also K. Derry & T.I. Williams, *A Short History of Technology: From Earliest*

Times to 1900 (Courier Dover Publications, 1993), fig. 102, p. 227. The earliest surviving clock which incorporated a fusee is the *Burgunderuhr*, a very early chamber clock apparently made for Philip the Good, Duke of Burgundy about 1430, now in the Germanisches Nationalmuseum, Nuremburg.

18. White, pp. 126–127.
19. Museum Willet-Holthysen, Herengracht 605, Amsterdam.
20. Freemantle's Specification, Patent No. 1737, AD 1790. Intellectual Property Office.
21. Webster, p. 819.
22. Webster, p. 819.
23. Eveleigh, p. 16.
24. Shorter's Specification, Patent No. 3075, AD 1807. Intellectual Property Office.
25. There are three surviving trade cards which describe or illustrate Marriott's Patent Jack. They are all in the British Museum Print Room collection – BM 85.94, 85.95 and 85.189.
26. Trade card formerly in the collection of Sarah Sophia Banks (1744–1818) sister of Sir Joseph Banks and collector of printed ephemera, BM 85.95.
27. Anne French et al., *John Joseph Merlin The Ingenious Mechanick* (Greater London Council, London, 1985), p. 79. The other Marriott jacks are in the York Castle Museum and the Museum of London. The latter was removed from the Mansion House, which is interesting as Marriott's trade card states he was 'the Furnishing Ironmonger to the Honorable Corporation of London'.
28. Johann Zoffany, *David Garrick in the Farmer's Return*, oil on canvas, 1762, Paul Mellon Collection.
29. Lane's Specification, Patent No. 4585, AD 1821. Intellectual Property Office.
30. Pearse's Specification, Patent No. 4693, AD 1822. Intellectual Property Office.
31. Peter Brears, *The Old Devon Farmhouse* (Devon Books, Tiverton, 1998), p. 131.
32. Webster, p. 819.
33. Eveleigh, p. 15.

CHAPTER FIVE

BARMS AND LEAVENS – MEDIEVAL TO MODERN

Laura Mason

Barms and leavens are both substances which contain cultures of organisms commonly known as yeast. Until the mid-nineteenth century they were routinely used in Britain to ferment flour mixtures and raise bread. Their use required skill and care, and was subject to social and economic nuances rooted in differing capacities for raising flour from different cereal species.

Barm, a frothy liquid, was taken from fermenting beer and was partially fermented malt liquor containing live yeast. Fast-acting and relatively easy to use, it is now rarely employed in baking except experimentally by food historians, but a yeast species, *Saccharomyces cerevisiae* is derived from this tradition and still provides commercial yeast for brewing and baking. Leaven could mean any substance added to dough to raise it, but is used in this paper to indicate dough reserved from one baking session to raise the next batch. Leaven is still used, for instance in some continental European baking and, as a runny mixture known as sourdough, in the USA. Yeast species contained in leavens vary according to the environment and those from the genus *Candida* are often present, together with other microbes responsible for the characteristically sour flavour.

Yeasts generally are single-celled organisms which metabolize carbohydrates in the presence of moisture and air, and excrete alcohol and carbon dioxide. Strains particularly suited to different activities have been selected for current use, hence terms such as brewers' yeast and bakers' yeast; the former requires little air and lots of food, rapidly producing large amounts of alcohol; the latter flourishes best with lots of air and moderate amounts of food, growing fast and producing little alcohol. This, however, was a development of the nineteenth century, and until then, both brewers and bakers were, to some extent, at the mercy of local microflora.

Long practice had taught early bakers something that science only unravelled in the twentieth century: that barms and leavens both act well on the proteins specific to wheat flour, but other cereals, especially rye, contain different proteins which respond better to the more complex microflora of leavens, whose inherent sourness aids fermentation in these grains.

Barm and leaven have the same net effect when used in baking wheat flour: incorporated into it with extra liquid, the yeasts they contain begin to break down starch to sugar and then to alcohol, in the process releasing carbon dioxide; their action, combined with kneading, encourages formation of a protein complex, gluten, peculiar to wheat, which is elastic and traps the gas, and baking preserves this light, spongy structure. Leaven gives extra flavour to wheat breads, but conveys no advantages over the use of barm. On the other hand, barm would be wasted in non-wheat doughs whose proteins do not form gluten. In these, a spongy structure equivalent to that of wheat bread is impossible to achieve, but acid leaven acts on their chemistry, especially that of of rye flour (and on wheat/rye mixtures in which rye is over 20 per cent of the total), to produce a texture closer to that of wheat bread. The action of leaven is complex and dependent on many factors including presence of oxygen, temperature, and water hardness as well as local microflora. Leavens used in the past must have varied greatly and the exact nature of their products will probably always remain something of a mystery.

THE ORIGINS OF BAKING WITH BARM AND LEAVEN

Until the development of chemical leavening agents in the late eighteenth century, and compressed yeast in the mid-nineteenth, barm or leaven were the only raising agents available: for light bread one or the other was needed. Either substance could be used alone, although barm was sometimes used to boost leaven. The origins of their use are lost in antiquity and related to the history of brewing. Brewing and baking were both known to the ancient Egyptians; there are numerous biblical references to leaven, and the classical Greek and Roman worlds both knew leavened bread.

To the Romans, brewing was a barbarian practice which they regarded as a northern European habit. Given this, bread made with barm may have been known in Britain from an early date, but exactly when has to be speculation. However, Ann Hagen (1998) commented on Anglo-Saxon words used for yeast including *beorma*, perhaps etymologically connected with *breowan*, to brew, which may have referred to fermented liquor from brewing, i.e. the substance later known as barm. She also mentions an Old English term for yeast, *dærst*, derived from *dros* (dregs), and speculates that it indicated a type now known as bottom-fermenting yeast or *Saccharomyces carlsbergensis* (used in low-temperature fermentation of light Continental beers and lagers), which would have given a slower-acting culture.[1] Elizabeth David remarks this type of yeast gives a heavier, damper, sourer bread than fast-acting barm taken from the top of fermenting liquor.[2] Hagen also speculates on terms which may indicate sourdough-type leaven or refer to yeast dried for longer keeping. Well before the Norman Conquest, then, it seems that the use of barms and leavens was known in England, and was a complex subject.

EARLY REFERENCES TO BARMS, LEAVENS, YEAST

The terms barm, leaven, sourdough and yeast were all recorded in English by the late Middle Ages. The *Oxford English Dictionary* cites barm in three quotes before 1400,[3] and gives an example of its use from the *Liber Cocorum* (c.1420) as an ingredient in a batter 'with egges and flour in batere þou make, put barme þer to'. Early quotes about leaven refer (sometimes figuratively) to its sour flavour 'ase þe leuayne zoureþ þet dogh' (1340) and 'He is the levin of the brede, which soureth all the past about'; a third (1471) to the use of leaven with wheat flour, and another (1483) mentions making 'levayne at every bache.' The last quote can be related to practice later recorded, of reserving a piece of dough at each baking. Quotations about leaven over the centuries must be treated with care, as the word was also used as a verb referring generally to raising dough.

The phrase sour dough was also used as early as the fourteenth century. The *OED* gives quotes from 1303 and 1398; the latter reads 'sowr dogh reseþ paste and brede þt is medled þerewiþ'. Quotes continue through the fifteenth and sixteenth centuries, but then it seems to vanish except as a dialect word. Presumably the expression remained in use in north America.

Quotes referring to yeast also come early, apparently as early as *c*.1000 in the Anglo-Saxon leechdoms. In later usage, the word yeast was firmly linked with barm, especially the sediment which settles out of it after a few hours. A term for yeast which was used in the Middle Ages, but which has completely vanished, was *goddisgoode* 'bicause it cometh of the grete grace of God'.

By the time comprehensive records appear in the late sixteenth century, practical application of barms and leavens related principally to the grain used for flour, and to a lesser extent to personal taste and economic circumstances. In turn this usage could be extended to the relative status of bread flours, with wheat as the choicest grain for high-quality breads of the type known as pandemayn and manchet in the fifteenth and sixteenth centuries. Although no really early records for how to make these survive, two recipes for manchet were printed at the end of the sixteenth century in *The Good Huswife's Handmaide for the Kitchin* (1588). One calls for 'a pinte of yest' (i.e. barm) alone; the other for a combination of leaven and yeast.[4] From the start of the seventeenth century, printed recipes show that barm was firmly linked with white wheat flour, rapidly raised to make high-status bread, fancy breads and cakes. Gervase Markham's instructions (1615) for making three types of bread clearly showed distinctions in quality, the use of barm, and two methods relating to leaven. He wrote 'Your best and principall bread is manchet' which was made in a clean kimnel with the finest flour 'and opening the flower hollow in the midst, put into it of the best Ale-barme the quantity of three pints to a bushel of meale…' Cheate (household) bread required a coarser wheat flour in a clean tub, trough or kinmell, kneaded with a piece of sour dough saved from a former baking, mixed with warm water and kneaded into the flour. Finally, a coarse brown bread was made for servants using mixed grain flour in a kneading trough which was only scraped, not washed, leaving fragments of leaven and yeast cells in the wood.[5]

BREWING, BAKING AND BARMS

To understand the use of barm, one must also consider brewing. 'As we brew, so we must bake' runs an old English saying, illustrating the close link between these two activities. Gervase Markham includes both actions in one chapter, *Of the Office of the Brew-house and the Bake-house*. Brewing generated ample supplies of barm, and household brewing and baking sessions must have been planned for the same time. This ready availability of barm for fine and fancy breads perhaps is at the root of the idea of 'cakes and ale' – both produced at the same time from the fast-working barm, and a source of enjoyment against the background of a plainer quotidian diet.

The technicalities and development of brewing affected the quantity and quality of barm available for baking over time. Until the mid-eighteenth century brewing was carried out both domestically, and by individuals who brewed for profit. Household brewing seems to have taken place about once a month, although some seasons were recognized as better than others. Winter cold slowed the process and summer warmth hastened it. Ale, the common drink of the English in the Middle Ages, was based on a simple process: malted barley was mashed (soaked) in hot water to extract soluble sugars; the liquid, now called wort, was drained off and fermentation started by adding a little barm. The fermenting liquor was beaten at intervals over twenty-four hours, and then tunned; once fermentation was complete the ale was consumed in a relatively short space of time. Barm for baking presumably was taken from the ale during those first twenty-four hours.

Any addition of flavourings to ale was regarded as adulteration. However, during the fifteenth century, the use of hops to flavour malt liquor became increasingly common, and the result was differentiated by the name of beer (a word apparently used interchangeably with ale in English up to the fifteenth century[6]). Andrew Boorde, in the mid-sixteenth century, said that ale should contain nothing more than malt, water and yeast, and that 'Ale for an Englysshe man is a naturall drynke', whereas 'Beer is made of malte, of hoppes and water; it is the naturall drynke for a Dutche man. And nowe of late dayes it is moche vsed in Englande to the detryment of many Englysshe men…'[7] Beer required the wort to be boiled with dried hops, then cooled to blood heat before yeast was introduced. Markham, in his brewing instructions, says that the barm should be mixed with wort kept back from before the hops were added. This yeasted wort was put in a large wooden bowl which was placed in the bottom of the fermenting vessel; the hopped wort was run gently on to it.[8]

Markham also comments that at the time he was writing, although some people did not put any hops in ale, the best brewers did add a small quantity. The use of hops in malt-based drinks spread unevenly and gradually across Britain in the following two centuries. Even in the eighteenth century, a distinction between the two was still being made. For instance, in *The Art of Cookery made Plain and Easy* (1747), Hannah Glasse gives recipes for beer and ale; both include hops but the proportion in the ale recipes is smaller. The distinction was vanishing by the nineteenth century, when a fashion for extremely well hopped, bitter brews developed. Hops act as a preservative (allowing beer to keep longer than ale); more importantly for the baker, they give a bitter taste. The change to brewing with hops affected the flavour of barm, a theme which recurs in cookery books over the eighteenth and nineteenth centuries.

Baking, then, was closely linked with supplies and quality of barm. To obtain barm, one had to know someone else who had some, for instance a neighbour. William Ellis, in *The Country Housewife's Family Companion* (1750) mentions a community which had a practice of sharing yeast: when one housewife brewed, she gave some barm to a neighbour for baking and brewing, so they rarely had to buy any.[9] This practice must have been an extremely ancient one.

One could buy barm from those who brewed commercially, in which case price as well as quality became a consideration for both domestic and commercial bakers. (The cost of yeast was one of the items included in bakers' 'allowances' – overheads – in calculations made by the Assize of Bread when fixing the size of loaves.) Ellis said that the price of barm fluctuated according to the weather, and could be expensive during cold spells 'even in some towns, where in warm weather it is cheaply and easily had for three-pence or four-pence a quart, and yet in hard and long frosts it is sometimes sold for six-pence, a shilling, two shillings, and I have known it sold for two shillings and six-pence a quart, in the great frost of 1740.'[10] He also indicated that brewers knew how to manipulate techniques to produce large quantities of yeast, and that in times of shortage, some individuals made barm to sell at a good profit.

Problems of supply during cold weather were recorded by William Holland, the vicar of Overstowey in Somerset who bought yeast for brewing and baking. On January sixteenth 1814, during very cold and snowy weather, he wrote, 'The frost being so severe we cannot get Barm for baking so that we are obliged to buy bread dear and sell wheat to the Poor cheap. I hope this will not continue, people do not care to brew this frosty weather which causes this scarcity of Barm.' The next day he wrote, 'We have got Barm at last and are busy baking.'[11] A. Edlin, in *A Treatise on the Art of Bread-Making* (1805), included an interview from 1804 with Mr Joseph Vere, Master of the Bakers' Company, who stated that the price of yeast had risen in the previous two years and to a regular sum of two shillings and seven pence a gallon[12]. An interview with a brewer revealed 'great and quick' seasonal fluctuations in the price of yeast, especially in 1797, from one shilling and sixpence a gallon to two shillings and sixpence a gallon. The delivery man was paid three-halfpence per gallon sold.[13]

Despite these fluctuations, vending of barm by brewers continued through the nineteenth and into the twentieth century. Whilst preparing this paper, I found that one of the *OED* quotes about barm came from *Sons and Lovers*, in which D.H. Lawrence mentions someone 'looking down the alley for the barm-man.' The *OED* also supplies a quote from 1925 about 'the man who sold barm drove round the district … one saw women hastening over the heath, jug in hand, to catch the "barm man".' My father could remember purchasing barm from a vendor who used to transport it in a can from the local brewery (in Ilkley) around outlying farms in the early twentieth century, and the family house possessed a small glazed earthenware jug, always known as the barm pot.

The best bakers took their yeast supply very seriously indeed, and some generated their own yeast. Edlin described the method used by Mr Gillispie, a baker at Leith. Essentially, he made an unhopped wort which he allowed to begin fermenting, returning the frothy barm which bubbled over the top of the vat three times, until it was 'of the thickness that good yeast ought to be.… it is an expensive and troublesome way of procuring it, but Mr Gillispie finds that a quart of it will go as far as a gallon of distillers' yeast.'[14] (Distillers' yeast, a subject not closely examined in this paper, became increasingly important in the nineteenth century.) Eliza Acton, in *The English Bread Book* (1857), records that some first-class London bakers even bought up yeast from mild home-brewed ale from small farms.[15]

QUALITY AND FLAVOUR IN BARMS

In early-modern recipes for breads, fruit cakes (and until the end of the seventeenth century, fritter batter) barm or ale yeast is a usual ingredient. The terms seem to have been interchangeable, and 'good ale yeast,' 'new ale yeast,' or 'a pint of good yeast' is often stipulated. New yeast would be livelier than that from a batch which had almost finished fermenting, working more swiftly on the bread. 'Good', used as a qualifier may simply have meant yeast which was working vigorously, but barms could lose strength or become infected with undesirable microbes, and methods for correcting this were recorded.

In *The London and Country Brewer* (1750), instructions are given '*To cure bad Yeast*. Add to it a little Flour, Sugar, Salt, Brandy and Beer, and it will bring it into a Fermentation ready to work new Beer or Ale Wort with. This mixture will also improve strong Drink Grounds, and make it fit to brew or bake with, instead of good Yeast.'[16]

Other eighteenth-century works expand on this; for instance, Martha Bradley (1756) who instructed:

> Put into a Marble Mortar a Spoonful of Sugar, a Tea Spoonful of Bay Salt, and Half a Spoonful of Flour; grind all these together, and when they are in fine Powder, and well mixed, put in half a Gill of Brandy, and a Quarter of a Pint of Beer; grind them all well together, then put in a little of the bad Yeast; grind and mix it all very well, and then bring in more by Degrees till all the Yeast is in.
>
> When it is all mixed, work it well, and pour it out into a Pan; set it in a warm Place covered, and in an Hour it will be fit to use.
>
> It exceeds the very finest Yeast unprepared, for the working of Beer or Ale Wort; and it may be also used for another very good purpose, which is to mix with strong Beer Grounds, for fitting it for Service. The Grounds with this Addition are just as good as common Yeast for the Service of Baking, or common Brewing; only it requires to stand a longer Time in a warm Place after all is mixed.
>
> These are Secrets not commonly known, and they may be of Use on many Occasions in fermenting Liquors for the Still, and to the Bakers; they are very innocent as may be known from the Ingredients, all of which are perfectly wholesome.[17]

Recipe writers also mention thick ale yeast, and yeast which is neither thick nor thin; evidently there were numerous subtle differences and opinions over what worked best. Eliza Acton remarked, in a discussion about yeast from home-brewed ale, that 'Experienced bread-makers … are enabled by long practice, to judge the effect which it will produce in any form.'[18]

Barm taken from hopped wort produces a bitter flavour in bread which was disliked by many people. Ellis (1750) described how northerners, accustomed to heavy, coarse, brown or oatmeal breads carried their own bread south with them to Hempsted 'to prevent their being forced to eat our *Hertfordshire* wheaten bread, saying – They do not like such a corky, bitter sort; – for you must know that in these Northern Counties, their yeast is mostly saved from strong mild ale, and not from strong hopped beer.'[19] The quantity of hops used was also seasonal; in the early nineteenth century, more was used in summer, to prevent the beer souring.[20] The specification of ale yeast in early modern recipes probably contained the assumption that it would be less hopped. Whilst brewing was still undertaken domestically, or on a local scale, bitterness could be controlled to some extent by requesting barm from less hopped brews.

As brewing became a more commercial enterprise in the mid-eighteenth century, guaranteeing less hopped barm must have become more difficult, and recipes for removing bitterness become more frequent. Ellis suggests several methods. The first was to wash it by covering it with cold water. After 24 hours much of the yeast sank to the bottom of the container, and the water, with some of the bitterness, was poured off. This method was the one most frequently recommended by domestic cookery writers, but it was only partially successful. A hundred years later, Eliza Acton, in *Modern Cookery for Private Families* complained:

> The yeast procured from a public brewery is often so extremely bitter that it can only be rendered fit for use by frequent washings, and after these even it should be cautiously employed. Mix it, when first brought in, with a large quantity of cold water, and set it by until the following morning in a cool place; then drain off the water, and stir the yeast up well with as much more of the fresh: it must again stand several hours before the water can be poured clear from it.[21]

Washing yeast also rendered it more solid, so that smaller quantities were required, and it could be more accurately measured;[22] judging the action of a tablespoon of sediment was easier than a pint of rapidly working barm.

A second method for washing, recommended by Ellis in 1750, was 'the common bakers way [which] is, to put long bran on a linen cloth, and your bitter yeast on that, which you are to wash out from the bran with hot water.'[23] In the mid-nineteenth century Anne Cobbett in *The English Housekeeper* (1851) was still recommending a variant on this: 'Put the yeast to the water you use to mix the 'batter,' or as the country people call it, 'set the sponge,' and stir into it 2 or 3 good handfuls of bran; pour it through a sieve or jelly bag (kept for the purpose), and then mix it into the flour. The bran not only corrects the bitterness of the yeast, but communicates a sweetness to the bread.'[24] She also suggested to 'put into the yeast 2 or 3 pieces of wood coal, stir them about, pour the water in, and then strain it.'[25] Ellis wrote that using skimmed milk in mixing the bread could also help the flavour.[26]

Eliza Acton considered that none of the expedients commonly recommended for removing bitterness worked, although stirring the white of an egg into the washing water sometimes helped 'but as gentian and various other powerfully-flavoured ingredients are partly substituted for hops in brewing the bitter beer which at present finds so much favour with the English public … it is extremely difficult to make bread with it that is free from bitterness.' She particularly disliked porter-yeast: 'from its dark colour, and its flavour also, [it] is objectionable for bread.'[27]

The distinction between ale and beer barm seems to have vanished by the early nineteenth century, and bakers transferred allegiance to barm from brewing small beer (probably similar to that known as 'mild' in the twentieth century). In 1829 William Kitchiner gave six bread recipes 'written by Mr Turner, Bread and Biscuit Baker, corner of London and Fitzroy Street, Fitzroy Square' most of which call for 'thick small beer yeast'.[28] Anne Cobbett also favoured small beer yeast as 'the best for making bread, as ale, or strong beer yeast is generally too bitter.'[29]

The colour of barm was remarked on as early as the mid-eighteenth century by Hannah Glasse, who stipulates in a recipe for 'muffings and oatcakes' ale yeast 'from pale Malt if you can get it, because it is the whitest'.[30] Problems of colour and flavour were still recognized in the twentieth century, when Edmund Bennion remarked that 'Brewers' yeasts carry with them the marks of their origin, for the slight flavour of hops is only removed with difficulty.'[31] He said they worked at a relatively slow speed, producing relatively small-volume loaves, with a slight darkness in colour and bitterness in flavour.

Possibly, where brewing was frequent, barm based on sweet, unhopped or lightly hopped wort may have been maintained, at least in the seventeenth and early eighteenth centuries. Evidence for this is slight, but in 1615 Markham specified that when brewing some unhopped wort should be mixed with the barm whilst the remainder was boiled with hops for brewing. This may have been a purely practical measure, in that the barm would have time to start working whilst the rest boiled but it would also be a time when barm with a sweeter flavour could be abstracted for baking. It is not clear if this is what happened, but some people obviously were fussy about the contexts in which hopped yeast was used. John Evelyn recorded a recipe for blackberry or elderberry wine which required 'new Ale yest without Hops'.[32] William Ellis commented on '*How the* London French *Bakers supply the Use of Yeast*', saying '…the *French* Bakers in *London,* who make the nicest and finest of bread, to avoid the ill taste and bad quantity of yeast, use a mixture of the first wort immediately from the malt, with some fine wheat flower and whites of eggs, for making *French* bread, and gingerbread.'[33] Alternatively, as Edlin recorded in 1805, bakers could use the absolute minimum of barm or brewers' yeast in an initial sponge (a portion of flour mixed with barm, yeast or leaven and liquid, left to start working before the rest of the flour was added and kneading commenced), then adding flour and water in increments until the desired volume of dough was achieved.[34]

KEEPING BARM AND YEAST

Given that barm could be expensive, supply intermittent and quality unpredictable, it is not surprising that methods for preserving yeast were devised. Washing barm and allowing it to form a sediment (essentially yeast cells) was a step towards preservation. Ellis suggested that the sediment could be put in a pitcher or bottle and covered and kept cold in a cellar, pond, well, or hole in the ground, which would inhibit activity in the yeast. Acton claimed that it could be preserved for some time under cold water:

> By changing this daily in winter, and both night and morning in very hot weather, the yeast may be preserved fit for use much longer than it would otherwise be; and should it ferment rather less freely after a time, a *small* portion of brown sugar and a little warm milk or other liquid, stirred into it a quarter hour or twenty minutes before it is required for bread-making, will restore its strength.[35]

Longer-term methods were suggested. Ellis instructed the housewife to pour off the thin liquid and dry the thick part, mix it with salt and shape into rolls, which he asserted would keep for a month. Another was to paint the yeast onto a board, let it dry, keep it in a dry place and scrape off some as required.[36] Hannah Glasse gave a detailed description of this:

A Method to preserve a large Stock of Yeast, which will keep and be of Use for several Months, either to make Bread or Cakes.

When you have Yeast in Plenty, take a Quantity of it, stir and work it well with a Whisk until it becomes liquid and thin, then get a large wooden Platter, Cooler or Tub, clean and dry, and with a soft Brush lay on a thin Layer of the Yeast on the Tub, and turn the Mouth downwards that no Dust may fall upon it, but so that the Air may get under to dry it. When that Coat is very dry, then lay on another Coat, and let it dry, and so go on to put one Coat upon another, till you have a sufficient Quantity, even to two or three Inches thick, to serve for several Months, always taking Care the Yeast in the Tub be very dry before you lay more on; when you have occasion to make Use of this Yeast, cut a Piece off, and lay it in warm Water, stir it together, and it will be fit for Use.[37]

Yet another method was to use a bundle of twigs. Glasse said:

if [the barm] is for Brewing, take a large handful of Birch tied together, and dip it into the Yeast and hang it up to dry, take great Care no Dust comes to it, and so you may do as many as you please, and when your Beer is fit to set to work, throw in one of these, and it will make it work as well as if you had fresh Yeast; you must whip it about again in the Wort and then let it lie, when the Fat [vat] works well, take out the Broome and dry it again, it will do for the next Brewing.[38]

Ellis also quoted this method, claiming '…though the yeast be bitter, the air will dry and freshen it against the next baking, when it may be washed in warm water.'[39]

In the twentieth century, John Kirkland in *The Modern Baker and Confectioner* (1931) suggested making dried yeast cakes. 'These consist of a large proportion of yeast mixed with fine corn or barley meal, cut into round biscuits about ¼ inch thick, and then very carefully sun-dried. Similar sorts of cakes were known and in use in this country quite a hundred years ago. They are still manufactured in America, and are in use in places where it is impossible to obtain a supply of fresh yeast.'[40]

Recipes for 'making' yeast appeared. Many required starting with a little live yeast and are really methods for increasing quantities of viable yeast. Ellis indicates that these methods were known to bakers by 1750. By the early nineteenth century, Mrs Rundell (1821) instructed how to make yeast on a domestic scale:

> Thicken two quarts of water with fine flour, about three spoonfuls; boil half an hour, sweeten with near half a pound of brown sugar; when near cold, put into it four spoonfuls of fresh yeast in a jug, shake it well together, and let it stand one day to ferment near the fire without being covered. There will be a thin liquor on the top, which must be poured off; shake the remainder and cork it up for use. Take always four spoonfuls of the old to ferment the next quantity, keeping it always in succession.[41]

Another method was to add a cupful of yeast to partially cooled mashed potato, which would take two or three hours to be ready. Isabella Beeton gave a recipe to make yeast for bread, which was essentially brewing, producing a small amount of hopped wort, which was yeasted and allowed to work for a few hours. Her instructions to put it into half-pint bottles ('ginger-beer bottles are the best for the purpose') and tie down the corks, so that the yeast 'will keep good for a few weeks' must have been hazardous, with much potential for exploding bottles if the yeast was on the lively side. She reckoned one bottle was sufficient for 18 lb of flour and, when required for use, instructed a mash of potatoes and flour be made and 'put in the yeast, pour it in the middle of the flour, and let it stand warm on the hearth all the night, and in the morning let it be quite warm when it is kneaded. The bottles of yeast require very careful opening, as it is generally exceedingly ripe.'[42] The hops, perhaps, were there for their preservative qualities, or possibly they were simply considered a natural part of the brewing process by this time; the recipe does seem to ignore the potential for producing a sweeter, unhopped yeast. Edlin also gives methods based on both potatoes and flour, and also tells how the Edinburgh bakers generated a leaven, or sponge, by making a paste of flour and water with yeast when commencing bread making.

This still doesn't answer the question of how one starts if one has no yeast at all. The answer is that wild yeasts are naturally present in the environment and will set up home in any suitable medium left exposed to the air; with luck they will be appropriate for brewing and baking. This method is still used by a few traditional breweries in Belgium, which produce beers of a type known as *lambic* or *gueuze*, with a curious sour flavour. However, Edlin says that bread with barm 'unless it is improperly prepared is never sour.'[43] This is in contrast to that prepared with leaven, which is characteristically sour.

LEAVEN

References to leaven in the literature can be confusing because of the general application of the word to raising dough, and the extension of its use, evident by the early nineteenth century, to the sponge. What is clear, is that by the seventeenth century, leaven in the sense of dough reserved from a previous baking as a sole means of adding yeast, was reserved for coarse types of bread by those for whom acquiring barm was not a problem. Leaven is slower acting than barm, has lesser raising power and gives a distinctive flavour in wheat bread. This, plus the association with coarse non-wheat breads made for servants or labourers, strongly suggests that as a raising agent it was less well liked and considered to be of a lower social status. It may have been slower acting and less predictable than barm, but had the advantage in that it was relatively easy to preserve.

The (scant) eighteenth-century evidence about use of leaven alone for raising wheat in English usage points towards it as more common among poor people. Ellis claimed that 'Leaven … is […] chiefly prepared for saveing yeast',[44] specifically mentioning that the labourer's wife who gave him information about it used this method 'as her money was short, and yeast sometimes scarce and dear.' She was baking 'flower'[45] (flour, without a qualifier, in English is usually wheat). Another factor which might have influenced a choice of leaven in the eighteenth century was a decline in the habit of home brewing and thus a decline in the availabilty of barm in smaller communities. But the use of leaven was apparently not widely known; Ellis also remarked that 'As many are ignorant of what leaven is, I shall in the first place give an account of it…'[46] He described how the labourer's wife, who baked about every 10 days 'always took care to save a piece of her leavened dough, at each baking, about the bigness of her fist, and making a little hole in the middle of it with her finger, ram'd it full of salt, and in a ball shape she let it lie covered over with salt in her salt-box till the next baking; by which time it got dry and hard…'[47] Another informant said to knead a piece of dough (of barley, or barley and rye) with salt, 'as long as it will take up any, then hang it up, or leave it covered with salt…'[48] Since early references to leaven given in the *OED* imply that it was well known – sufficiently so to be a metaphor for sourness of human character – ignorance of its use may have been a relatively recent development.

To use leaven, the yeast it contained had to be revived and encouraged to work, a process which took several hours. Again, Gervase Markham gave good detail on early seventeenth-century methods, in a type of bread known as cheate made from coarser wheat flour than manchet:

> take a sowre leauen, that is a peece of such like leauen saued from a former batch, and well fild with salt, and so laid up to sower, and this sower leauen you shall breake into small peeces with warme water, and then straine it, which done, make a deepe hollow hole … and therein power your strained liquor [i.e. hot water]....[49]

Some of the flour and liquor were mixed together to batter consistency, more flour sprinkled over the top, and the whole left overnight (the process which later became known as 'setting a sponge'). In the morning, more warm water was added, with some barm and salt, and the mixture kneaded.

The use of leaven mixed with barm in some circumstances seems to have been normal; perhaps it was because a certain proportion of leaven added an interesting flavour to wheat bread, as well as reducing expenditure on barm. 'Lady Graies' manchet in the 1590s called for it; Markham's cheate bread has already been noted, and Ellis records how crumbled leaven mixed with half a pint of yeast and warm water, was poured it into the middle of the flour and left to ferment. Ellis seems to have preferred a combination of leaven and yeast for raising bread, remarking that 'half the usual quantity of yeast suffices, and yet causes the bread to eat pleasanter, to be hollower, and is wholsomer than if the dough was all made with yeast. On which account the *French* and other foreigners commonly make their bread with some leaven in it.'[50]

Boosting leaven with barm was not strictly necessary. A 'Receipt for making Bread without Barm, by the help of a Leaven,' originating from the Dublin Society was copied by Hannah Glasse, and is informative about quantities:

> Take a Lump of Dough, about two Pounds of your last making, which has been raised by Barm, keep it by you in a wooden Vessel, and cover it well

with Flour. This is your Leaven; then the Night before you intend to bake, put the said Leaven to a Peck of Flour, and work them well together with warm Water. Let it lye in a dry wooden Vessel, well covered with a Linnen Cloth and a Blanket, and keep it in a warm Place. This Dough kept warm will rise again next Morning, and will be sufficient to mix with two or three Bushels of Flour, being worked with warm Water and a little Salt. When it is well worked up, and thoroughly mixed with all the Flour, let it be well covered with the Linen and Blanket, until you find it rise; then knead it well, and work it up into Bricks, or Loaves, making the Loaves broad, and not so thick and high as is frequently done, by which means the Bread will be better baked: Then bake your Bread.

Always keep by you two or more Pounds of the Dough of your last baking, well cover'd with Flour to make Leaven to serve from one baking Day to another; the more Leaven is put to the Flour the lighter and spongier the Bread will be, the fresher the Leaven, the bread will be less sour.'[51]

Most recipes relied on leaven which had originally been started with barm, but this was not absolutely necessary. The process of capturing wild yeast is simple in principle, and must have been known from the start of brewing and baking, but there are few written instructions for it. Edlin, in 1805, did tell how to start a leaven without barm:

…a longer space of time is required to accomplish the fermentation and a different mode of mixing must here be pursued. A small quantity of flour and water are mixed together, and allowed to remain several hours covered up. …fresh flour and water are added to this dough as soon as it is perfectly sour, and allowed to ferment and rise, when more flour and water must be added at stated intervals, till a sufficient quantity is ready for baking. A great deal of nicety is required in conducting this operation, for if it is continued too long the bread will be sour, and if too short a time has been allowed for the dough to ferment and rise, it will certainly be heavy.[52]

He describes his own experiment in making a leaven from scratch with flour and water, finding that after 36 hours a paste of flour and water to be 'in a complete state of fermentation … it was also of a sourish taste.' After adding more flour, water and some salt, kneading, allowing it to ferment another six hours and then adding a little more flour and baking in loaves he had bread which 'looked porous, was tolerably light, ... the taste was sourish ... but still it was palatable.'[53]

PROBLEMS IN USING LEAVEN

Difficulties of working with leaven are illustrated by the comments about loaf size, texture and flavour. Ellis said that the dough should be 'kneaded all into a moderate stiffness; for if it was kneaded too soft, the bread would be apt to spread in the oven, be light and crumble; and if too stiff kneaded, it may be baked till it is too close, heavy, hard.'[54] Pricking holes in the top of the loaves, 'with a pocket meat fork, or something else' apparently helped to give the loaves a better finish 'for this lets out the air when the bread begins to be hot in the oven, that otherwise would cause the upper crust to be puffed up and crack.'[55] Edlin, too, commented on the need for careful mixing.

The sourish flavour in bread using leaven is derived from lactobacilli which develop as the paste ages, contributing an acid flavour (hence the term sour dough). They are also responsible for other uncertainties of quality, especially in wheat bread, as they tend to grow faster than the yeasts, inhibiting their action, and weakening gluten, both leading to closer-textured bread. Problems in other doughs were recorded by Ellis, whose informant, a servant maid from Cheshire, was accustomed to baking with barley, or half barley, half rye flour using salted leaven. 'She said, they make no use of yeast, unless they think the leaven not strong enough to ferment the dough of itself.... The staler the leaven the closer will be the bread, and the sooner sour, and if the dough is not well kneaded, it will be streaky.'[56] Leaven, like barm, was susceptible to spoilage organisms which adversely affected flavours and textures.

Used alone or together, the choice of barm and leaven must have been dictated by the type of flour baked, region, economics and personal taste, and related to brewing practices and availability of barm as well. One reason the French may have favoured leaven could have related to production of alcoholic drinks, and lesser availability of barm from brewing. In a discussion of John Evelyn's translation of the bread section of Nicolas Bonnefons *Les Delices de la Campagne* (1654), William Rubel observes that 'what makes French bread *French* ... is a methodical approach to mixing and leavening dough for the purpose of controlling flavour and texture, paired with a reliance on sour dough, *levain*, rather than ale yeast, *levure*, for leavening.'[57] Evelyn's translation of Bonnefons does mention barm, but it is clear that leaven was more important; this was probably related, at a practical level, to the fact that wine making was more important in most of France than brewing. Wine yeasts are adapted to ferment grape juice, a very different substrate to malted worts, and must be far more seasonal, principally available in autumn during the vintage, unlike beer yeasts which were replenished through the year by regular brewing. The 'methodical approach' is essential for good results when using leaven; barm, provided it is working well, is a more forgiving agent.

SOUR TROUGHS

One method for preserving leaven, probably of great importance in terms of the proportion of the population who relied on it, but for which few references survive, was the sour trough used with flour from cereals other than wheat. This was a wooden kneading vessel which was scraped, not washed, after kneading so that fragments of dried dough containing yeast clung to the wood and contributed to leavening the next batch of dough. In 1615 Markham tells that:

> For your browne bread, or bread for your hinde servants which is the coarsest bread for man's vse, you shall take of barly two bushels, of pease two pecks, of wheat or rie a peck, a peck of mault; these you shall grind altogether and dress it through a meal siue, then putting it into a sower trough set liquor [water] on the fire, and when it boils, let one put on the water, and another with a mash-rudder stir some of the flower with it after it hath been seasoned with salt and so let it be till the next day, and then putting to the rest of the flower, worke it vp into a stiffe leauen, then mould it and bake it into greate loaues with a verie strong heate: now if your trough be not sower enough to sower your leauen, then you shall either let it lie longer in the trough or else take the helpe of a sower leauen with your boiling water…[58]

Ellis, too mentions how in some parts of Yorkshire a blackish rye bread was eaten, 'here they employ leaven in common to make their bread, and as their kneading-tub has always part of this leavened dough sticking to it, it contributes towards leavening and fermenting the next dough.'[59] Baking this way evidently continued into the early nineteenth century. Tuke in his *General View of the Agriculture of the North Riding* (1800) gave a more detailed description, saying that:

> ...formerly, a very black, heavy, sour bread was made of rye, and is not yet entirely out of date, among the lower orders of the country; it is made in the following manner: a large tub, called a kimlin, is provided; this being only scraped, and not washed out, after each time of using, the paste which remains on the sides becomes sour; in this vessel about one half of the meal intended to be used, is mixed with water in the evening; this is covered up with some dry meal, and lies in sponge till morning; in that time, the tub has communicated its acidity to the whole mass, which causes a fermentation similar to that produced by yeast; it is then worked up stiff with the remainder of the meal.

Tuke remarked that it was made in large quantities, 'three bushels at a baking is frequent, which quantity is made into seven or eight loaves: many farmers do not make this bread more than four, or six times in the year.'[60] Bread made this way would also keep a long time. With care and luck, yeast cultures contained in leaven could be kept going for months or years (in modern times, there are reports of carefully maintained sourdough cultures being perpetuated for decades, particularly in the USA). Sour troughs must have had a long history but their lower-class associations mean that few records of their use survive.

THE INTRODUCTION OF COMPRESSED YEAST

The baking trade and most domestic bakers in Britain must have given up completely on the idea of sour leaven in the mid-nineteenth century, by which time they seem to have applied the word leaven to the initial sponge of yeast, water and flour. They were also giving up on barms, as a new form of yeast was introduced from Holland. This was distillers' yeast, a by-product of spirit production, at first known as German yeast and the forerunner of compressed yeast. Eliza Acton reported that:

> This has very generally superseded the use of English beer-yeast in London, and other places conveniently situated for receiving quickly and regularly the supplies of it which are imported from abroad; but as it speedily becomes putrid in sultry weather, and does not in any season remain good long

after its arrival here, it is unsuited for transmission to remote parts of the country.[61]

She was impressed with it; only a small, easily measured quantity was needed, an ounce for a quartern (half a gallon, or three and a half pounds) of flour. Mixing required some nicety:

> The yeast should be very gradually and perfectly moistened and blended with the warm liquid; for unless this is done, and the whole rendered as smooth as cream, the dough will not be of the uniform texture which it ought, but will be full of large hollow spaces, which are never seen in well-made bread. … A leaven may be first laid with the yeast, and part of the liquid when it is preferred, as directed for bread made up with beer-yeast, but the result will be equally good if the whole be kneaded up at once, if it be made *quite firm*.[62]

German yeast quickly became popular, but in its turn was replaced by compressed yeast specifically for bakers produced in dedicated factories. Distillers' yeast worked rapidly at high temperatures, ideal for baking, and bakers' yeast, too, was chosen for these qualities.[63] Brewers still produced massive quantities of yeast, but quality was less reliable. The barm-man made his rounds in some localities, but there was still an excess from which they were desperate to profit. In 1913, Walter A. Riley reported that 'as a rule, for every barrel of beer brewed, about 3 to 4 lbs of yeast is wasted'.[64] But bakers no longer wanted it. 'Many endeavours have been made, and numerous patents have been brought out, in order to make brewers' yeast suitable for bakers. It is to some extent the fault of the brewers themselves that they have lost this profitable outlet, for the bakers have seldom been treated properly, any old yeast being given to them. It is the author's experience that if the yeast is selected for them they often prefer brewers' yeast.'[65] Help was at hand for the brewers; the development of a process known as autolysis allowed their waste yeast to be made into a new product, Marmite. Specially produced bakers' yeast was reliable, of uniform quality, and relatively inexpensive, all factors which must have made it popular with both commercial and domestic bakers.

Compressed yeast shared with barm the fact that it did not keep well for long periods; it would swiftly dry out, or become cheesy or rotten.

Attempts to develop dried yeast were aimed at overcoming this. Florence White said in 1932 that 'those who live in "out of the way" places of the Empire may be glad to know that "Royal Yeast Cakes" (a Canadian product) can be sent anywhere, properly packed for tropical and semi-tropical climates, by the Army and Navy Stores.'[66] Bennion remarked that whilst it was readily available and exported for use in hot countries, 'In practice it is found that a considerable amount of the fermenting power is destroyed, and at least the same weight of such yeast [i.e. as fresh compressed yeast] must be used in any formula if adequate aeration is to be obtained in the resultant bread.'[67] Good dried yeast did not become widely available until some decades later.

CHEMICAL AGENTS

Although chemical raising agents – now represented for the home baker by baking powder, or a mixture of bicarbonate of soda with an acid such as buttermilk – work by a completely different action to yeast, bakers both commercial and domestic experimented with them. They are relative newcomers in the long history of baking, only dating back to the late eighteenth century. Pearlash, or potash, was an alkaline substance generated by burning plant material; it reacts with acid substances to produce carbon dioxide. Also used was hartshorn, produced by distillation of deer antlers to give a substance which releases ammonia and carbon dioxide on heating to 140°F. Other chemical raising agents became the subject of experiments at the end of the eighteenth century. Edlin remarks on the use of naturally occurring gaseous mineral waters, such as Seltzer water, to make light bread, or, in England, 'the artificial Seltzer water prepared by Mr Schweppe'. He had high hopes for their development: 'all these waters are well known to be highly impregnated with fixed air, and whoever can concentrate this air in sufficient quantity to mix with flour, may make as light a bread as any baker with yeast, and in no respect will it shew a test of acidity.'[68] One of his recipes includes instructions for making 'artificial yeast' by impregnating a flour paste with gas generated by powdered marble and sulphuric acid,[69] a process which sounds dubious from the health and safety point of view, although Eliza Acton commented that muriatic (hydrochloric) acid worked far better in combination with bicarbonate of soda than did tartaric acid. She was working at the point when chemical leavening agents really became viable. Commercial baking powder was introduced around 1850, but did not become lastingly popular for making bread (it staled quickly) in Britain, although the ABC Bread Company in late nineteenth-century London used a patented process of chemical leavening. Eventually, the amount of yeast used in bread was in turn much reduced and the necessity for slow fermentation almost rendered obsolete by the development of the Chorleywood process of short-time bread making in the early 1960s. This produced the spongy, long-keeping yeast-leavened loaf which British consumers continued to demand.

Baking and brewing are now two entirely separate activities, their historic links broken by a science devoted to controlled production of cultured yeasts. No-one, viewing the shelves of wrapped sliced white loaves in a supermarket, or the plethora of bread buns and rolls all generated from the same basic doughs made by intensive mixing and short fermentation time, would now think of the care with which bakers once nursed pots of working barm or worried about supply during cold weather. Centuries of care and skill which went into using barms were lost as easier alternatives replaced them, although our modern concept of bread, relying on white wheat flour quickly raised with yeast, derives from the high-status manchets of late medieval and early modern England.

Likewise, the native tradition of leaven appears to have entirely vanished, together with the prudent housewives who made salt-preserved leaven to save a few pence on buying barm. With it has gone a wide range of regional, non-wheat breads which would have been fascinating to us in their variety of shape, flavour and texture, although those who had to subsist on them might not have felt affectionately about them. The idea of leaven has undergone a slight revival since the 1970s under influence from continental Europe and the USA. A wider appreciation of the flavours and textures derived from the use of sour leavens, coupled with hints at possible health benefits, have led to more interest in this method among a few craft bakers, something to be welcomed in the homogenized world of plant bakeries.

NOTES

1. Ann Hagen, *A Handbook of Anglo-Saxon Food: processing and consumption* (Hockwold-cum-Wilton, Anglo-Saxon Books, 1998), pp. 15–16.
2. Elizabeth David, *English Bread and Yeast Cookery* (London, Allen Lane, 1977), p. 98.
3. *Oxford English Dictionary*, 2nd edition, accessed online March 2005.
4. Anon. *The Good Huswifes Handmaide for the Kitchin* (London, 1588).
5. Gervase Markham, *The English Huswife* (London, 1615), pp. 126–7.
6. John Burnett, *Liquid Pleasures: a social history of drinks in modern Britain* (London, Routledge, 1999), p. 112.
7. Andrewe Boorde, *A Compendyous Regyment or a Dyetary of Helth* edited by F.J. Furnivall (London, Early English Text Society, 1870), p. 256 .
8. Markham, op. cit., p 122.
9. William Ellis, *The Country Housewife's Family Companion*, from the edition of 1750 with an introduction by Malcolm Thick (Blackawton, Prospect Books, 2000), pp. 58–9.
10. Ellis, op. cit., p. 57.
11. *Paupers and Pig Killers. The diary of William Holland, a Somerset parson 1799–1818*, edited by Jack Ayres (Stroud, Sutton Publishing, 1995), p. 258.
12. A. Edlin, *A Treatise on the Art of Bread-Making*, transcribed and introduced by Tom Jaine from the edition of 1805 (Blackawton, 1992), p. 96.
13. Edlin, op. cit., pp. 99–100.
14. Edlin, op. cit., p. 71.
15. Eliza Acton, *The English Bread Book Bread Book*, from the edition of 1857 with an introduction by Elizabeth Ray (Lewes, Southover Press, 1990), p. 92.
16. Anon. *The London and Country Brewer*, attributed to William Ellis (London, 1750), p. 294.
17. Martha Bradley, *The British Housewife*, from the edition of 1756 with an introduction by Gilly Lehmann (Blackawton, Prospect Books, 1996), vol. VI, p. 369–70 .
18. Acton, 1990, p. 93.
19. Ellis, op. cit., p. 53.
20. Edlin, op.cit., p. 42.
21. Eliza Acton, *Modern Cookery for Private Families*, from the edition of 1855 with an introduction by Elizabeth Ray (Lewes, Southover Press, 1993), pp. 491 –2.
22. See Acton, 1990, pp. 92–3.
23. Ellis, op. cit., p. 58.
24. Anne Cobbett, *The English Housekeeper*, a facsimile of the 6th edition of 1851 (East Ardsley, EP Publishing Ltd, 1973), p. 268.
25. Cobbett, ibid.
26. Ellis, op. cit., p. 63.
27. Acton, 1990, p. 93.
28. William Kitchiner, *The Cook's Oracle*, 7th edition (London, 1829), pp. 475–7.
29. Cobbet, op.cit., p. 268.
30. *The Art of Cookery Made Plain and Easy by a Lady* (Hannah Glasse); a facsimile of the first edition of 1747 (London, Prospect Books, 1983), p. 151.
31. Edmund Bennion, *Breadmaking: its principles and practice* (London, Oxford University Press, 1939), p. 32.
32. Christopher Driver, ed., *John Evelyn, Cook* (Totnes, Prospect Books, 1997), p. 133.
33. Ellis, op. cit., p. 258.
34. Edlin, op. cit., pp. 42–3.
35. Acton, 1993, p. 492.
36. Ellis, op. cit., p. 54.
37. Glasse, op. cit., p. 151.

38. Ibid.
39. Ellis, op. cit., p. 58.
40. John Kirkland, *The Modern Baker and Confectioner: a new and revised edition* (London, The Gresham Publishing Company, 1931), vol. I, p. 82.
41. Maria Rundell, *A New System of Domestic Cookery by a Lady* (London, John Murray, 1821), p. 242.
42. Isabella Beeton, ed., *Beeton's Book of Household Management* (originally published 1859–61; London, Chancellor Press enlarged edition published 1982), p. 839.
43. Edlin, op. cit., p 35.
44. Ellis, op. cit., p. 60.
45. Ellis, op. cit., p. 59.
46. Ibid.
47. Ibid.
48. Ellis, op. cit., p. 62.
49. Markham, op. cit., pp. 126–7.
50. Ellis, op. cit., p. 60.
51. Glasse, op. cit., p. 151.
52. Edlin, op. cit., p. 30.
53. Edlin, op. cit., pp. 37–38.
54. Ellis, op. cit., p. 59.
55. Ellis, op. cit., p. 60.
56. Ellis, op. cit., p. 62.
57. William Rubel, 'Parisian Bread circa 1654', in *Petits Propos Culinaires* 77 (Blackawton, Prospect Books, 2004), pp. 9–11.
58. Markham, op. cit., p. 127.
59. Ellis, op. cit., p. 54.
60. John Tuke, *A General View of the Agriculture of the North Riding* (London, 1800), p. 118.
61. Acton, 1993, p. 494.
62. Ibid.
63. Bennion, op. cit., p 32; Kirkland, op. cit., vol. I, pp. 81–2.
64. Walter Alfred Riley, *Brewery By-Products* (London, Brewing Trade Review, 1913), p. 101.
65. Riley, op. cit., p. 103.
66. Florence White, *Good Things in England* (London, Jonathan Cape, 1932), p. 62. White suggested that 2 tablespoons of barm were about equivalent to 1 oz of compressed yeast for anyone wishing to experiment with recipes.
67. Bennion, op. cit., p. 35.
68. Edlin, op. cit., p. 31.
69. Edlin, op. cit., p. 70.

CHAPTER SIX

BAKING IN A BEEHIVE OVEN

Susan McLellan Plaisted

This paper is a compilation of research on the firing and use of the wood-fired beehive oven and of experiential research with the actual firing of over twenty-six different beehive ovens, both original and reproduction, in the United States. The baking tradition in America evolved from its European roots. As the colonists arrived on the eastern shores, there were no bake-ovens. The native Americans were preparing mixtures of maize (corn) and water and baking on stones. As the English arrived and created settlements, their goal was to clear land and plant wheat. Unlike maize, wheat contains gluten and the European methods and technology of baking evolved to exploit and enhance the properties of this material. Baking technology came to America with European wheat. In what is now the State of Virginia, over 200 fragments of a seventeenth-century gravel-tempered clay oven, known to be unique to Britain and produced in the Devon potteries at Barnstaple, were found.[1] This type of oven was typically sixteen inches high at the crown and sixteen inches across at the widest point with one-inch-thick walls. In England, these were the common bread ovens in west-country cottages. They were built into the side wall of the open hearth so that only the opening was visible from the front. At Jamestown, Virginia, the oven is thought to have been fired outside under a wooden protective structure. Most beehive ovens found in seventeenth-century England were significantly larger in size than the Devon clay oven. Typically, the English oven was of circular domed construction, built in one of the hearth walls, could measure three or more feet in diameter and had a small rectangular access opening. Hannah Glasse in *The Art of Cookery Made Plain and Easy* wrote:

> In the building of your oven for Baking, observe that you make it round, low roofed, and a little Mouth; then it will take less fire, and keep in the

Heat better than a long oven and high roofed, and will bake the bread better.[2]

In 1851, the author of *Modern Domestic Cookery* wrote that ovens,

> should be round, not long; the roof from twenty to twenty four inches high, the mouth small, and the door of iron to shut close. This construction will save firing and time, and bake better then long and high-roofed ovens.[3]

Original historic ovens surveyed in New York State have been classified according to their shape: oval, three-sided, and barrel vaulted. The most common oven is the oval-shaped dome and the deepest ovens are of this type and can be fifty to sixty inches in depth.[4] The position of the beehive oven in the American hearth demonstrates an evolutionary trend. During the eighteenth century, when it was common for the hearth to be a large walk-in structure and wood was more abundant, the oven was built into the back wall and the smoke vented into the fireplace chimney. The next position was the oven located in the side wall of the hearth, necessitating the cook to pull her embers from the oven with her back to the main fire. The final position of the oven placed the mouth of the oven flush with the face of the hearth. This location required a flue built into the mouth of the oven to prevent smoke from entering the kitchen.

Whatever the location of the oven, whether in the main kitchen hearth or a bakehouse, most were of similar construction. The oven generally used in Count Rumford's time (1753–1814), and still used in country houses and by some modern bakers, is 'an arched cavity of brick with a flat brick floor'.[5] This cavity was closed by a door which in its most primitive form could be a tile or slab of stone, set in place with clay or dirt. In *Modern Domestic Cookery* by A Lady (1851), it is written,

> For the baking of bread there can be no doubt the fire-proof brick oven is the best. Brick ovens are also the best for baking all kinds of large cakes and pies; the reason of which is chiefly owing to their being generally capable of retaining the heat a much longer time than one built of iron; unless indeed, when the latter happens to be very substantially made of wrought iron.[6]

Eliza Acton wrote about the brick oven:

> Much of the quality of bread depends on its being well baked, and therefore, the nature and construction of the oven used for it, when it is required in large quantities, are very important. Of all that are in common use amongst us at present, a brick oven, heated with wood, is generally considered as the best adapted to it...[7]

In Philadelphia, Sarah Josepha Hale wrote in 1857 that,

> a brick oven, heated with wood, is far superior to any other for baking bread, as well as for most other purposes, being much more easy to regulate, as well as more economical, than an iron one.[8]

In 1885, W. Mattieu Williams in *The Chemistry of Cooking* comments: 'Baked clay is an excellent radiator, and therefore the surface of bricks forming the arched roof of the oven radiates vigorously upon its contents below, which are thus heated at top by radiation from the roof, and at bottom by direct contact with the floor of the oven.'[9] The Genesee County, New York, survey of brick ovens dating from 1789 to 1860, documented that the doors used to seal the baking chamber are rarely located. Wooden doors, because of their insulating properties, hold the heat better than metal, but no original wooden doors were found. Four ovens in the survey had hinged cast-iron doors which were attached to the exterior opening of the oven and equipped with damper openings to allow the door to remain closed while the oven was being fired.[10] But for many ovens, the door was typically left open so that sufficient oxygen could maintain the fire and also for the smoke to escape through the front aperture into the main chimney.

The fuel was of primary importance in the firing of a beehive oven so that the heat produced would be sufficient for a baking day. Eliza Acton commented: 'I have known a very large brick oven, heated in the middle of the day with one full sized faggot or rather more, and a log or two of cord-wood, which was added when the faggot was partly consumed, still warm enough at eight or nine o'clock in the evening to bake various delicate small cakes, such as macaroons and meringues, and also custards, apples, &c'.[11] She noted that 'when there is no cord-wood at hand, the large faggot-stems can be used instead, but will not have so good an effect'.[12] Elm, beech or oak were considered the best cord-wood. Esther Copley describes in *The Complete Cottage Cookery* that,

> The fuel for heating an oven should be very dry, and such as will heat through quickly. The stalky part of furze, and the brush-wood of faggots answer the purpose best. If larger wood is used (such as beech spokes and billets they should be split into pieces about the thickness of a spade-handle. Coals are altogether improper; and so are the knotty roots or greenwood.'[13]

Faggots were bundles of light branches as dry hawthorn, which when 'bound into faggots…and burnt in ovens…be soon kindled in the fire, and give a strong light, and sparkleth, and cracketh, and maketh much noise, and soon after they be brought all to nought.'[14]

Eliza Acton further comments on the way to heat a large brick oven.

> Lay a quantity of shavings or other dry light fuel into the centre of the oven, and some small branches of faggot-wood upon them; over these place as many of the larger branches as will make a tolerably large fire, and set light to the shavings. As the wood consumes keep adding more, throwing in, after a time, amongst the live embers the stout poles of the faggot, and, lastly, two or three moderate-sized logs of cord-wood, when the oven is of large dimensions and the heat is wanted to be long-sustained. When no cord wood is at hand, the necessary quantity of large faggot or other wood must be used instead.[15]

Mrs Hale of Philadelphia wrote that 'If a brick oven be a good one, it will heat sufficiently in an hour.' She recommended to 'kindle the fire with some quick burning material, then fill it up with hard wood, split fine and dried; let the wood burn down, stir the coals evenly over the bottom of the oven, and let them lie there till they are like embers.'[16]

Note the reliance on the seemingly abundant wood supply in America as faggots were not typically used, nor has this writer had experience with the use of faggots. Esther Copley estimates that 'from one hour to an hour and a half is the time required for heating an oven.'[17] Larger ovens required more time, 'from an hour and a half to two hours will be required to heat thoroughly a full-sized bake oven.'[18] 'But, observe, the longer the time elapses between the heatings of an oven, the longer it takes to bring it to a sufficient heat.'[19] The actual amount of time of firing depends on the both the size of the oven, the types of items to be baked, and the duration of baking desired.

The judgment of when the oven was completely fired was one of the chief elements to the skill of beehive-oven baking. 'Nothing but experience can give aptitude and exactness in determining the proper heat.'[20] One indication was if during firing the flames had been licking the roof of the oven or had achieved a bloom in the oven. Some bakers used a method of rubbing a twig across the dome of the oven and if sparks flew the heating was sufficient. Another indication was the burning off of the soot. 'When the oven is sufficiently hot, the bricks at the arch and sides will be clear from any color of smoke.'[21] Initially, the bricks turn black when a fire is built in the oven, but as the temperature rises, the carbon burns off, first the dome, then the sides, and finally from the back. This is the indicator that the oven is fired that the author has found most satisfactory.

When the oven had retained sufficient heat for baking, it was time to draw out the remaining embers and ashes from all parts of the oven to the mouth. A tool, called a rooker, made of iron and resembling the letter L fixed to a long wooden handle, was first used for this purpose. This was followed by the use of the oven hoe. The hoe was also made of iron fixed to a handle and was used to scrape out the ashes that had escaped the rooker. The final step was to use a swabber or mawkin (essentially a long handled mop) to swab out the final ashes and leave the oven floor slightly damp.[22] This moisture, combined with the natural vapour generated by the dough itself, created the atmosphere of steam so important in successful bread baking. The next important phase is the equalization of heat in the oven. 'To ensure a sufficient degree of heat to bake bread properly, and a variety of other things in succession after it when they are required, the oven should be well heated, then cleared and cleansed ready for use, and closely shut from half an hour to an hour, according to its size. It will not cool down as it would if the baking were commenced immediately after the fire was withdrawn.'[23] In addition, this writer has found from experience that the temperature of the oven rises significantly if the bread is loaded in the oven without this step.

If an oven is fired properly, the initial temperature is hotter than that required for the baking of bread. The heat is stored in the bricks of the oven and this heat diminishes slowly over time. If the temperature is too hot when the bread is put in, the smell of burned bread will soon be in the air. There were methods used in England for testing the temperature of the oven which are documented in primary sources, 'To ascertain whether a brick oven be heated to the proper degree for baking bread, it is customary for persons who have not much experience to throw a small quantity of flour into it. Should it take fire immediately, or become black, the oven is too hot, and should be closed, if the state of the dough will permit it to wait, until the temperature is moderated: this is better than cooling it down quickly by leaving the door open. It may also be tested by putting into it small bits of dough about the size of walnuts, which will soon show either it be over heated or not sufficiently so.'[24] This writer prefers not to put flour on her oven floor but tests the oven with her arm. The article 'Brick Ovens in the Genesee Country, 1789–1860: Architectural and Documentary Evidence' presents this technique: 'Traditionally, the temperature is tested by placing the bare arm in the oven and counting until the heat forces the baker to retract the arm.'[25] Actually, the baker learns to feel the different levels of heat to bake all food items at the appropriate degree of heat.

The heat required for baking was stored in the walls of the oven and diminished slowly over time. The amount of heat retained depended on the construction materials of the oven and the firing method employed. By the sixteenth century, a sequence had evolved in the order of baking to maximize the use of the oven heat. Coarse, wholegrain breads (cheat bread) were baked first, followed by white breads (manchets), coffins (joints of meat in pastries or pies), and then great cakes, cakes and finally items in patty-pans. The residual or slack heat of the oven was used for twice-baked breads, drying fruits or for confectionery. In *The Good Housewife's Jewel* (1596), Thomas Dawson describes the baking of the bread in his receipt 'To make fine biscuit bread': 'Then let it into your oven, being so hot as it were for cheat bread.'[26] He gives another example of twice-baked bread: 'And when you will occupte [make use] of it, slice it thin and dry it in your oven, your oven being no hotter than you may abide your hand in the bottom.'[27] For meat pies Dawson gave these instructions in his receipt 'To make a pie': 'Your oven must be very hot as the first, that your pies will keep a great while, the longer you keep them [in the oven] the better they will be.'[28] Gulielma Maria Springett Penn (first wife of William Penn) wrote in her manuscript receipt book under 'Too Make Naple Biskitts', 'bake them in an oven as heated for manchets'[29] and under 'Too Make

Puffs' she wrote, 'then put them in an oven, after pyes, you must be sure the oven bee not too hott.'[30] Sir Kenelm Digby collected receipts which included 'To make a cake', an example of a great cake with 'eight wine quarts of flower.'[31] The directions proceed,

> Then get a tin hoop that will contain that quantity, and butter it well, and put it upon two sheets of paper well buttered; so pour in your Cake, and so set it into the oven, being quick that it may be well soaked, but not to burn. It must bake above an hour and a quarter; near an hour and half. Take then a pound and half of double refined Sugar purely beaten and searsed; put into the whites of five Eggs; two or 3 spoonfuls of rose-water: keep it beating all the time, that the Cake is a baking which will be two hours; Then draw your Cake out of the oven, and pick the dry Currants from the top of it: and so spread all that you have beaten over it, very smooth, and set it a little into the oven, that it may dry.[32]

Returning the great cake to the oven after having been iced sets the icing nicely. 'Another very Good Cake' is included in Digby's collection of receipts for cakes and states, 'Let your oven be of a temperate heat, and let your Cake stand therein two hours and a half.'[33] The baking day ends with a slack oven, which is a temperature suitable for this receipt, 'To make Cracknels', from *The Compleat Cook* (1655) by W. M.: 'lay them upon buttered Papers, and when they go up into the Oven, prick them, and wash the top with the yolk of an Egg beaten, and made thin with Rose-water or fair water; they will give with keeping, therefore before they are eaten, they must be dryed in a warm oven to make them crisp.'[33]

NOTES

1. Elizabeth David, *English Bread and Yeast Cookery* (new American edition, Biscuit Books, 1994), illustration 18 between pp. 98, 99.
2. Hannah, Glasse, *The Art of Cookery Made Plain & Easy*, facsimile of 1796 edition (United States Historical Research Service, 1994), p. 354.
3. John Murray, ed., *Modern Domestic Cookery* (London, 1851), p. 577.
4. Peter Benes, ed., *Foodways in the Northeast,* The Dublin Seminar for New England Folklife Annual Proceedings, 1982, p. 70.
5. David, op. cit., p. 168.
6. Murray, p. 577.
7. Eliza Acton, *The English Bread Book*, transcription of 1859 edition (Lewes, Southover Press, 1990) p. 97.
8. Mrs. Sarah J. Hale, *Mrs. Hale's New Cook Book* (Philadelphia, 1857), p. 422.
9. David, p. 168.
10. Benes, p. 72.
11. Acton, p. 97.
12. Ibid.
13. David, p. 175.
14. Peter Brears, *All the King's Cooks: The Tudor Kitchens of King Henry VIII at Hampton Court Palace* (Souvenir Press, 1999), p. 43.
15. Acton, p. 98.
16. Hale, p. 422.
17. Quoted in David, p. 175.
18. Acton, p. 98.
19. Quoted in David, p. 175.
20. Ibid.
21. Hale, p. 422.
22. A. Edlin, *A Treatise on the Art of Bread-Making*, transcribed and introduced by Tom Jaine from the edition of 1805 (Blackawton, the editor, 1992), p. 73.
23. Acton, p. 97.
24. Ibid, pp. 98, 99.
25. Benes, p. 64.
26. Thomas Dawson, *The Good Housewife's Jewel*, transcription of 1597 edition (Southover Press, 1996), p. 79.
27. Ibid.
28. Ibid. p. 67.
29. Evelyn Abraham Benson, ed., *Penn Family Recipes* (Trimmer Printing, 1966) p. 50.
30. Ibid. p. 53.
31. Sir Kenelm Digby, *The Closet of Sir Kenelm Digby Opened*, transcription of the 1669 edition, ed. Jane Stevenson and Peter Davidson (Totnes, Prospect Books, 1997), p. 181.
32. Ibid.
33. W. M, *The Compleat Cook and A Queens Delight*, facsimile of 1655 edition (Prospect Books, 1984), pp. 40, 41.

BIBLIOGRAPHY

Eliza Acton, *Modern Cookery* (London, Longmans, 1845).
——, *The English Bread Book*, from the edition of 1857, with an introduction by Elizabeth Ray (Lewes, Southover Press, 1990).
Ahmad Y. al-Hassan, *Taqi al-Din and Arabic Mechanical Engineering* (Institute for the History of Arab Science, Aleppo University, 1976).
Anon., printed broadside. Printed by David Hannot on the Ice, at the Maidenhead at Old Swan Stairs. 16 January 1716.
Anon*., Family Guide*, printed broadside (London, 1794).
Anon., *God's Works is the World's Wonder*, printed broadside (London, 1683).
Anon*., Great Britain's Wonder: London's Admiration*, printed broadside (London, 1684).
Anon., *The Good Huswifes Handmaide for the Kitchin* (London, 1588).
Anon*., The Jubilee of George the Third – the father of his people – an account of the celebration in the towns and villages throughout the United Kingdom of the forty-ninth anniversary of his reign, 25th October 1809* (Birmingham, 1810), also second edition (London, 1887).
Anon., *The London and Country Brewer*, attributed to William Ellis (London, 1750).
William Barnes, *Poems of Rural Life in the Dorset Dialect* (Kegan Paul, Trench Trubner & Co., 1879).
Isabella Beeton (ed), *Beeton's Book of Household Management,* originally published 1859–61 (London, Chancellor Press enlarged edition published 1982).
Peter Benes (ed.), *Foodways in the Northeast*, The Dublin Seminar for New England Folklife, Annual Proceedings, 1982.
Edmund Bennion, *Breadmaking: its principles and practice* (London, Oxford University Press, 1939).
Evelyn Abraham Benson (ed.) *Penn Family Recipes* (Trimmer Printing, 1966).
Frederick Bishop, *The Wife's Own Book of Cookery* (London, 1856).
Andrew Boorde*, A Compendyous Regyment or a Dyetary of Helth*, edited by F.J. Furnivall (London, Early English Text Society, 1870).
Martha Bradley, *The British Housewife* from the edition of 1756 with an introduction by Gilly Lehmann (Blackawton, Prospect Books, 1996).
Peter Brears (ed.) *Yorkshire Probate Inventories 1542–1689,* Yorkshire Archaeological Society, 1972.
——, *The Kitchen Catalogue* (Castle Museum, York, 1979).
——, *Traditional Food in Yorkshire*, John Donald, Edinburgh, 1987
——*, The Old Devon Farmhouse*. Devon Books (Tiverton 1998)
——*, All the King's Cooks*: *The Tudor Kitchens of King HenryVIII at Hampton Court Palace* (Souvenir Press, 1999).
Theo Brown, 'The Folklore of Devon', in *Folklore*, Vol. 75, No. 3 (Autumn, 1964).
The Builder, vol. IX, 1851.
Robert Burnard, *Transactions,* Devonshire Association. XVIII, 1896.
John Burnett, *Liquid Pleasures: a social history of drinks in modern Britain* (London, Routledge, 1999).
John Byng, *Byng's Tours – The Journal of the Hon. John Byng 1781–1792,* edited by David Souden (Century, London, 1991).
Noel Carrington and Clarke Hutton, *Popular English Art* (Penguin, London, 1945).
J.J. Cartwright (ed.), *The Travels Through England of Dr Richard Pococke*, vol. 1, Camden Society, Second Series 42, 1888.
Robert Chambers, *The Book of Days* (London, 1864).

D. Clinton (ed.), *The Court and Kitchen of Elizabeth Commonly Called Joan Cromwell* (London,1664; Cambridge 1983).
Anne Cobbett, *The English Housekeeper,* a facsimile of the 6th edition of 1851 (East Ardsley, EP Publishing Ltd, 1973).
Randal Cotgrave, *A Dictionarie of the French and English Tongues* (London, 1611).
Ian Currie, *Frosts, Freezes and Fairs* (Frosted Earth, London, 2002).
Thomas Dawson, *The Good Housewife's Jewel*, facsimile of 1597 edition (Southover Press, 1996).
Daniel Defoe, *Tour Through the Whole Island of Great Britain* (London, 1724–1727).
A. Edlin, *A Treatise on the Art of Bread-Making,* transcribed and introduced by Tom Jaine from the edition of 1805 (Blackawton, 1992).
Dennis Edwards and Ron Pigram, *The Romance of Metro Land*, Bloomsbury Books, London, 1979 and 1986.
Elizabeth David, *English Bread and Yeast Cookery* (London, Allen Lane, 1977).
K. Derry & T.I. Williams, *A Short History of Technology: From Earliest Times to 1900* (Courier Dover Publications, New York, 1993).
Sir Kenelm Digby, *The Closet of Sir Kenelm Digby Opened*, transcription of the 1669 edition, ed. Jane Stevenson and Peter Davidson (Totnes, Prospect Books, 1997).
Christopher Driver (ed), *John Evelyn, Cook* (Totnes, Prospect Books, 1997).
Ellis, William, *The Country Housewife's Family Companion*, from the edition of 1750 with an introduction by Malcolm Thick (Blackawton, Prospect Books, 2000).
David J Eveleigh, *Bogs, Baths & Basins* (Sutton, Stroud, 2002).
——, '"Put down to a bright clear fire" The English Tradition of Open Fire Roasting', in *Folklife*, 29 (Leeds, 1991).
John Farey, *General View of the Agriculture of Derbyshire*, 1813.
Anne French et al., *John Joseph Merlin The Ingenious Mechanick* (London, Greater London Council, 1985).
Hannah Glasse, *The Art of Cookery Made Plain and Easy by a Lady*, a facsimile of the first edition of 1747 (London, Prospect Books, 1983)
Henry Fielding, *Grub Street Opera* (1731).
John Ferguson, *Forged and Founded in Cornwall* (Cornish Hillside Publications, 2000).
John Florio, *Queen Anna's New World of Words* (London, 1611).
T. Garrett, *The Dictionary of Practical Cookery* (1893).
John Gay, *Trivia, Or, the Art of Walking the Streets of London* (London, 1716).
William Gilpin, *The Life of Bernard Gilpin* (Glasgow, 1830).
George Laurence Gomme, *Ethnology in Folklore* (London, 1892).
Francis Grose, A *Classical Dictionary of the Vulgar Tongue* (London, 1785).
Ann Hagen, *A Handbook of Anglo-Saxon Food: processing and consumption* (Hockwold-cum-Wilton, Anglo-Saxon Books, 1998).
S.J.Hale, *Mrs. Hale's New Cook Book* (Philadelphia, 1857).
C. B. Hieatt & S. Butler, *Curye on English* (Oxford, 1985).
William Holland, *Paupers and Pig Killers. The diary of William Holland, a Somerset parson 1799–1818*, edited by Jack Ayres (Stroud, Sutton Publishing, 1995).
Sir W. H. St.J. Hope, *Windsor Castle, An Architectural History* (1913).
Household Ordinances (Society of Antiquaries, 1790).
How We Build (Leamington Spa, Sidney Flavel & Co., n.d., c.1937).
The Illustrated London News, 13 November, 1847.
The Illustrated London News, 22 December, 1894.
William Hone, *The Every Day Book* (London, 1826).
Alexander Hunter, *Culina Famulatrix Medicinae* (York, 1806).
The Ironmonger, 5 April, 1879.
The Ironmonger, 31 March, 1900.

Johnson, & A. Greutzner, *Dictionary of British Artists 1880–1940* (Woodbridge, 1999).
Journal of the Royal Agricultural Society of England, vol. 12, 1851.
Pehr Kalm, *Visit to England 1748*, trans. by Joseph Lucas (Macmillan & Co., 1892).
William Kitchener, *Apicius Redivivus; Or, The Cook's Oracle* (London, 1817).
John Kirkland, *The Modern Baker and Confectioner: a new and revised edition* (London, The Gresham Publishing Company, 1931).
Patrick Lamb, *Royal Cookery* (1726 edition).
J.C. Loudon, *Cottage, Farm and Villa Architecture* (Longman, 1833, new edition, 1836).
Gervase Markham, *The English Huswife* (London, 1615).
Martineau & Smith's Hardware Trade Journal, 31 January, 1882.
Henry Mayhew, *London Labour and the London Poor* (London, 1851).
Mechanics Magazine, 17 October, 1846.
Mechanics Magazine, Saturday 22 July, 1848.
John S. Moore, *Frampton Cotterell & District Inventories* (Colchester, Phillimore, 1976).
Joseph Moxon, *Mechanick Exercises or the Doctrine of Handy-Works* (London, 1678).
John Murray (ed.), *Modern Domestic Cookery* (London, 1851).
Hermann Muthesius, *The English House*, trans. Janet Seligman (London, Crosby, Lockwood Staples, 1979; original first published Berlin, 1904–5).
W. M., *The Compleat Cook and A Queens Delight*, facsimile of 1655 edition (London, Prospect Books, 1984).
Notes and Queries, 6th Series, 7 (1883).
The Oldham Advertiser, 27 November, 1858.
Mildred Mastin Pace, *Friend of Animals: The Story of Henry Bergh* (New York, Charles Scribner's Sons, 1942).
Samuel Pepys, *The Diary of Samuel Pepys* edited by R. Latham and W. Mathews (London, Bell & Hyman, 1972).
P. A. S. Poole, ed., *A Cornish Farmer's Diary* (Penzance, the editor, 1977).
Frank Prager, *Brunelleschi: Studies of his Technology and Inventions* (Cambridge, MA, The M.I.T. Press, 1970).
Nicholas Reed, *Frost Fairs on the Frozen Thames* (Folkestone, Lilburne Press, 2002).
Robin Reilly and George Savage, *Wedgwood the Portrait Medallions* (London, Barrie & Jenkins, 1973).
Alfred Riley, *Brewery By-Products* (London, Brewing Trade Review, 1913).
Steve Roud, *The English Year* (London, Penguin, 2008).
William Rubel, 'Parisian Bread circa 1654', in *Petits Propos Culinaires* 77 (Blackawton, Prospect Books, 2004).
Maria Rundell, *A New System of Domestic Cookery by a Lady* (London, John Murray, 1821).
P. Sambrook. and P. Brears (editors), *The Country House Kitchen 1650–1900* (Stroud, Sutton, 1996).
Bartolomeo Scappi, *Opera* (Venezia, 1570).
R. Sherwood, *The Court of Oliver Cromwell* (Cambridge, 1977).
Mark Smith, 'The Oldham Miners' Strike Medallion', *NMMA Newsletter*, No. 21, Spring, 2001.
M. L. Stanton, J. B. Partridge and F.S. Potter, 'Worcestershire Folklore', in *Folklore*, Vol. 26., No. 1 (31 March, 1915).
The Stratford-on-Avon Herald, 17 October, 1907.
Benjamin Thompson, Count Rumford, *Essay on the Construction of Kitchen Fireplaces* (T. Cadell and W. Davies), 1799.
S. Minwel Tibbott, 'Going Electric: The Changing face of the Rural Kitchen in Wales', 1945–55, *Folk Life*, volume 28, 1989–90.
Barry Trinder and Geoff Cox, *Yeomen and Colliers* (Colchester, Phillimore, 1980).
Gabriel Tschumi, *Royal Chef* (London, 1954).

John Tuke, *A General View of the Agriculture of the North Riding* (London, 1800).
Thomas Turner, *The Diary of Thomas Turner 1754–1765*, edited by David Vaisey (Oxford, Oxford University Press, 1985).
A.P. Wadsworth and Julia L. de Mann, *The Cotton Trade of Industrial Lancashire 1600–1780* (Manchester, 1937).
J.H. Walsh, *A Manual of Domestic Economy* (London, Routledge, 1st edition, 1856).
Thomas Webster, *An Encyclopaedia of Domestic Economy*, 2nd edition (London, Longman Brown & Green, 1847).
Susannah Whatman, *The Housekeeping Book of Susannah Whatman 1776–1800* (Century, 1987).
Florence White, *Good Things in England* (London, Jonathan Cape, 1932).
Lynn White, *Medieval Technology and Social Change* (New York, OUP, 1966).
A. Willan, *Great Cooks and Their Recipes* (London, 1992).
John Wilkins, *Mathematical Magic* (London, 1648).
Lawrence Wright, *Home Fires Burning* (London, Routledge and Kegan Paul, 1964).
Pietro Zonca, *Novo teatro di machine ed edificii per varie e sicure operationi, cō le loro figure* (Padova, 1607).

INDEX

Figures in bold are page references to illustrations.
Cited authors are indexed by name, but titles of books are not indexed unless the work is anonymous.

Acton, Eliza, 34, **121**, 131–135, 143–145, 151, 152
Adam, James and Robert, 28
Aga cookers, 52
Albert Range, 50
ale, 128–135
American cooking stoves, 47, 49
American Stove Warehouse, Cheapside, London, 47
Arnott, Dr Neil, 45
Atkins, 'Cripple', 55, 56

barley, 129, 136, 138, 141
barm, 125ff.
Barnes, William, 23
Barnstaple, Devon, 149
baron of beef, see Lord Mayor's Day
Batley Carr, Yorkshire, **61**, **62**
beer, 125, 127, 129, 130, 132–134, 136–137, 142–144
Beeton, Isabella, 19, 36, 41
Benham & Sons, 47
Bennett, Alfred, jack-makers, Birmingham, 115, 120
Bennion, Edmund, 134, 145
Benthall Foundry, Coalbrookdale, **22**, 28
Berthoud, Ferdinand, chronometer maker, 112
Betchworth House, Surrey, **22**
Beverley & Wylde, Leeds, **39**, 46
Bishop, Frederick, 91
Bodiam, Sussex, 23
Bodley, George, iron founder, Exeter, 35, 36
Bologna, Italy, **58**, 68, 69
Bonnefons, Nicolas, 141
Boorde, Andrew, 129
bottle-jacks, **38**, 41, 107, **109**, 112, **113**, 115, 116, 120
Bourne, Thomas, scale-maker, Birmingham, **106**
Bradley, Martha, 132
Braithwaite, Joseph, **113**
bread making, 125ff.

brewing, 125–138, 140–142, 144
Bridgewater, Duke of, 75
Bristol, Clifton, Harley Place, **22**, 28, **39**
Brown and Green, stove makers, Luton, **40**, 49
Brown, J., 92
Brown, Theodora, 65
Bruges Stove, 46
Brunelleschi, Filippo, 108
Buckland-in-the-Moor, Devon, 64
Bucklebury Foundry, 28
Bucklebury Manor, Berks, **21**, 28
bull roast, see ox roast
bull running, Stamford, 63
bull running, Tutbury, 63
Bunsen, Robert Wilhelm, 45
Burney, Frances (Fanny), 102
Byng, John (Viscount Torrington), 23

Carême, Antonin, 90
Carrington, Noel, 51
Carron Foundry Company, **22**, 28, 51
Carter, William, & Co, Birmingham, 42
Chambers, William, scale-maker, Birmingham, **106**
Charlton, Greenwich, Greater London, 66, 67
Chatsworth House, **105**
Chester, 72
Chipping Norton, Gloucs., 68
Clare, Peter, jack-maker, Manchester, 107
clockwork spits, 99ff.
closed ranges, **33**, 35, 36, **37**, **38**, **40**, 41, 42, 45
coal, seacoal, 20, 23, 24
Coalbrookdale Company, **26**, **33**, **34**, **38**, **43**
Cobbett, Anne, 133, 134
coke boilers, 52
Columbian Stove Company, 47
Compleat Cook, The, 155
Congresbury, Somerset, **30**
Constitutional Club, London, **79**

Copley, Esther, 152
Cornish ranges, **48**, 50, 51
Cosmopolitan Cooking Range, **38**, 47
Cottager's Stove, 47
Cox, James, 102, 108
Cruikshank, George, **58**, 60
Cutler, Albert, builder, 51

da Vinci, Leonardo, 108
dangle-spits, **2**, **38**, **79**, 100, **105**, 107, 116
David, Elizabeth, 127
Dawson, Thomas, 154
Deakin, Thomas, ironmonger, London, **29**, 46
Defoe, Daniel, 66
Defries, Nathan, gas engineer, 45
Deptford, Greater London, 67
Devon, 23, 36
Digby, Sir Kenelm, 155
distillers' yeast, 131, 143, 144
Dobbie, Forbes & Co., 47, 49
Dunham Massey, Cheshire, 75
Dyrham Park, Gloucs., 36

Eagle Range, **39**
Eagle Range and Foundry Company, Birmingham, 46
Ebernoe, W. Sussex, 67
Eccles, Lancashire, **62**
Economical Derby Range, 42
Edlin, A., 130, 131, 135, 137, 138, 140, 141, 145
Egerton, John, 72
Ellis, G.H., 42
Ellis, William, 130, 132–136, 138, 139, 141, 142
Emigrants Stove, 47
Evelyn, John, 135, 141

faggots, 151–152
Falkirk, Stirlingshire, 47
Farey, John, 31
Fawley, Hants, 69
Fielding, Henry, 83
Flavel, William, iron founder, Leamington Spa, 36, 51
Frampton Cotterell, Gloucs., 20
Freemantle, William, watchmaker, 112
frost fairs, 55ff.
furze as fuel, 24
fusee-jacks, 108, 111, 112, 115, 116, 120, **114**, **117**

Gainsborough, Thomas, 102

Garnons, Herefordshire, 71
gas and coal ranges, 45, 46
gas stoves, **39**, 51
Gay, John, 55
Gem portable range, **40**
Genesee County, New York State, 151, 154
George III, jubilee, 69, 71
German yeast, 143, 144
Gillispie, baker, Leith, 131
Gilpin, Bernard, 65
Gilpin, William, 65
Glasse, Hannah, 129, 134–136, 139, 149
gluten, 126, 141, 149
Gomme, Sir Laurence, 64
Good Huswife's Handmaide for the Kitchin, 128
Gould, Chester, **106**
Gourney, John, Master Cook of the King's Mouth, 84
grate, **21**
grates, 20, **21**, 24, 27
Greenwich, Greater London, 67
Griffier, Jan, the Elder, 56, **57**
Griffin Foundry, Derbyshire, 31
Grose, Francis, 67
Gunnersbury House Museum, 92
Gyles, Thomas, of Winterbourne, Gloucs., 20

Hagen, Ann, 126
Hale, Sarah Josepha, 151, 152
Hammond, Elizabeth, **118**, 120
Hampton Court, kitchens, 84, **85**, 87
Hardwick Hall, Derbys., 63
Harris & Kingdom, ironmongers, Bristol, **30**
Harrison, Joshua, stove-grate manufacturer, Derby, 42
hartshorn, 145
Hartwell House, Bucks., 71
Hattersley, iron founder, **37**
Hatton, Thomas, watchmaker, 111
Heathfield Hall, Handsworth, **21**
Herald Range, 45
Hill and Wilberforce, Messrs, 46
hiring fairs, 68ff.
  Chipping Norton, 68
  Shipston-on-Stour, 68
  Stowe-on-the-Wold, 68
  Stratford-upon-Avon, 68, **73**, **74**
Hodgson, Mr, butcher, 77
Hogenberg, Nikolas, **58**
Holland, Rev. William, 130
Holne, Devon, 64, 65

INDEX

Holyhead, 27
Hone, William, 63, 66
hops, 129, 130, 133–135, 137
horn fair, Charlton, 66, 67
horn fair, Ebernoe, 67
Houghton-le-Spring, Durham, 65, 66
Housekeeping Book of Susannah Whatman, 27
Hunter, Dr Alexander, 83

Improved Vertical Spring Roasting Jack, 112
Insall, Donald, and Associates, 97

J.D. Young, iron founder, Barnstaple, **40**
jacks, see bottle-jacks, dangle-spits, fusee-jacks, mainspring and fusee jacks, smoke-jack, spits, spring-jacks, steam-driven jacks, weight-jacks
Jamestown, Virginia, 149
Jeakes, Clement, **109**
Jibb, Joseph, Sleaford, 63
John Linwood's Improved Veruvolver, 120

Kalm, Pehr, 20, 99
Kea, Cornwall, **48**
Kent, William, 88
Kew Palace, kitchen, **85**, 88
Kings Weston, Gloucs, **25**, 31
Kingsteignton, Devon, 63–65
Kirkland, John, 136
kitchener, see closed ranges
Kitchiner, Dr William, 134

Lamb, Patrick, 88
Lane, William, jack-maker, Birmingham, **117**
Langmead, Joseph, iron founder, London, 32
Larbert Portable Range, 49
Lawrence, D.H., 131
Leamington Kitchener, 36
leaven, 125ff.
Leeds Gas Stove Works, **39**, 46
Lichfield Rage, 42
Linwood, John, jack-maker, Birmingham, 120
Livingstone Portable Range, 47
Lloyd, Edmond, ironmonger, London, **109**, 115
London and Country Brewer, 132
London, frost fair 1309, 55
    frost fair 1363/64, 55
    frost fair 1607/08, 55
    frost fair 1683/84, **54**, 56, **57**, 59, 60, 77
    frost fair 1714/15, **54**, 55, 59, 77

frost fair 1739, 60, 77
frost fair 1814, **58**, 59, 60, **61**
Lincoln's Inn Fields, Sir John Soane's House, **29**
Lord Mayor's Day, **76**, 78, **79**
Spring Gardens, 102
Longman, Green, Brown & Longman, publishers, 120
Lord Mayor's Day, **76**, 78, **79**
Loudon, J.C., 46, 47, 50
Louis XVIII, 71
Lowther Castle, Cumbria, **109**

mainspring and fusee jacks, 108, 111, 112, **114**, **117**
Malby and Sons, **114**
Markham, Gervase, 128, 129, 134, 139, 142
Marmite, 144
Marriott, Henry, ironmonger, Fleet Street, **2**, 116
Menager, M., chef, 95
Merlin, John Joseph, **101**, 102, 104, 107, 108, **110**, 111, 112, **113**, 115, 116, **117**, 119
Midland ranges, **43**, 49
miners' strike, Oldham, 1858, **68**, 75
Modern Domestic Cookery, 150
mops or hiring fairs, 68ff.
Moret, M., chef, 92
Moxon, Joseph, **98**
Munich, Germany, **30**, 35
Muthesius, Herman, 41

New York State, 150
Newark Cottage Range, 32
Nicholson, William, Newark, **29**, 32
Nicol, Richard, mason, 84
North Harrow, Middlesex, 52
Norwich, 78, **80**

Oldham, Lancashire, **67**, 75
open ranges, **30**, 32, 41, **43**, **44**
Osborne House, Isle of Wight, 95
ovens, 87, 92, 96, 107, 115
    beehive, 149ff.
    in ranges, 19ff.
Overstowey, Somerset, 130
ox roasts, 55ff.
    Batley Carr, **61**, **62**
    Chester, 72
    Fawley, 69
    Garnons, 71

Houghton-le-Spring, 65
Norwich, 78
Oldham, 75
Reading, 71
Stratford-upon-Avon, 68, **73**, **74**
Tamworth, **70**
Windsor, 69, **70**, 71, 77
paraffin stove, 51
Parks, Mrs William, 34, 36
Patricroft, Lancashire, **62**, **66**
Pearse, John, ironmonger, Tavistock, **118**, 119, 120
Penn, Gulielma Maria Springett, 154
Penzance, Cornwall, 24
Pepys, Samuel, 20, 100
Peters, William, and Son, Bristol, **121**
pig roast, Stratford-upon-Avon, **74**
Pococke, Dr Richard, 27
portable ranges, **40**, 46, 47, 49
Portreath, Cornwall, 50
potash, 145
Prize Kitchener, 45
purl, 60

Radcliffe, Thomas, iron founder, Leamington Spa, 45
ram roast, Buckland-in-the-Moor, 64
 Holne, 64, Holne, 65
 Kingsteignton, 63, 64, 65
Ransome S. & E., London, 47
Reading, Berks., 71
Reading, Abbot of, 55
Redruth, Cornwall, 50
Richard, Andrew, mason, 84
roast goose day, Norwich, **80**
roasting ranges, **85**
Robinson, Thomas, ironmonger, London, **26**, 31, 32
Rookhope, Stanhope, Co. Durham, **44**
Rotisseur Royal, **101**, 104, 107, 108, **110**, 111, 112, **113**, **114**, 116, 120
Rubel, William, 141
Rumford, Count (Benjamin Thompson), 23, 24, **30**, 35, 150
Runcorn Canal, 75
Rundell, Mrs, 137
Russells, Derby, 45
rye, 126, 138, 141–143

Scappi, Bartolomeo, 108, 111, **114**
Schweppe, Mr, 145

screen, roasting, 47, **79**, **86**, 91, 92, **93**, **94**, **101**, **106**, 107, **109**, 112, **113**, 115, 116, **118**, 120, **121**
Seaton Delaval Hall, Northumberland, 27
seltzer water, 145
Shipston-on-Stour, Gloucs., 68
Shorter, Edward, mechanic, London, 115, 116
Smith & Wellstood, Bonnybridge, 49
Smith, Mark, 77
Smith, Messrs Ebenezer, 31
Smoke Abatement Exhibition 1882, 45
smoke control, 45
smoke-jack, 89, 91, 100, 101, 104, 107, 116 , **109**, **113**
Smyth, Margaret, of Westerleigh, Gloucs., 24
sourdough, 125, 127, 128, 138, 140–143, 146
Soyer, Alexis, 45
spits, **70**, 84, 87–90, 92, 95, 96, 99ff.; see also dangle-spits
Spong, John, 100
spring-jacks, 99ff.
Stamford, Lincs., 63
Stanley Portable Range, 47
Stanton, L.M., 68
steam-driven jacks, 100, 107, **106**
Stephanoff, J., **86**, 89
Stevens, James, of Zennor, Cornwall, 23, 24
stoves, see ranges
Stowe-on-the-Wold, Gloucs., 68
Stratford-upon-Avon, Warws., 68, **73**, **74**
Strutt, Joseph, 107
Sutton in Ashfield, Notts, **48**
Swinton Range, **37**

Tamworth, Staffs., **70**
Telford, Salop, 20
Tschumi, Gabriel, 95, 96
Tuke, John, 142–143
turf as fuel, 24
Turner, Thomas, grocer, 23
turnspits, 84, 87, 88, 90
Tutbury, Staffs., 63

Underwood & Co., ironmongers, Bristol, **22**, **25**, 28

Vanbrugh, Sir John, **25**, 31
Vancouver, Charles, 23
Vere, Joseph, 130

Walker Iron Foundry, York, 50

INDEX

Walsh, J.H., **33**, 41
Watkins, Frank, **90**, 92
Watt, James, **21**
Webb & Sons, Messrs, 95
Webster, Thomas, 45, 115
weight-jacks, **98**, 99–101, **102**, **103**, 104, 108, **109**, 111, 112, 115, 116, **117**, 119, 120
West, Robert, of Knaresborough, 20
Wharton, Thomas, Lord, 20
wheat, 126, 127, 128, 130, 133, 135, 138, 139, 141, 142, 146
White, Florence, 145
Williams, W. Mattieu, 151
Windsor, Berks., 69, **70**, 71, 77

Windsor Castle, kitchens, 83ff., **86**, **89**, **90**, **93**, **94**
wood as fuel, 20, 23, 120, 151–152
Wright, Benjamin, 42
Writtle, Essex, 20
Wyatt, James, 69
Wyatville, Sir Jeffrey, **86**, 91yeast, 125ff.

Yorkshire ranges, **44**, 46, 49, 50
Young, William, 45

Zennor, Cornwall, 23–24
Zoffany, Johann, 119
Zonca, Pietro, 108, 111, **117**